THE TOP 1% LIFE

Advance Praise

"Kathleen sums up in her book the philosophies she has been teaching in our office for years. I could comment on the eloquent way she has presented the information, but instead I will talk about results. We spend over $150,000.00 a year on Lead Generation, and the only way our agents qualify, is by attending Kathleen Black's Training. I thought I needed to teach them a presentation, but Kathleen in her classes and her book really teach a philosophy for success. You need to understand these principles. Congratulations Kathleen!"

—**Paul Baron**, Owner, C21 Leading Edge Realty,
#1 Production Nationally for C21

"This is an incredible journey that you were able to convey in what felt like an authentic and powerful way. It is clear to me that you have a phenomenal growth mindset and are able to walk through a firestorm leading a team laughing on the other side of it.

The principles you are describing will resonate well with any business owner who wants to build a team and ultimately trade less of their own time for money. The team synergy you describe, the systems, the abundance mindset, trust and loyalty are all key cornerstones of high performing entrepreneurial teams when results win as opposed to politics.

And last but not least, your grit and relentless desire to build on your own terms shine through this book. Your ability to grow thick skin while the world around you was constantly trying to tear you down, and the sense of guilt for not always being able to show up for your kids the way you wish you could - these points in particular all resonate with female leaders."

—**Julia Bloom**, Innovation Leader, Agile Coach

"Having worked as a solo agent for 10 years and now as the Director of Sales on a successful Team that was coached by Kathleen's Team and systems, I can say first-hand, without a doubt that these systems are game changers! This book is a great resource for solo agents, aspiring and current team leaders looking to control their business rather than have their business control them. It is possible to grow a successful business and Team while still having time to enjoy and experience life! Thank you Kathleen!!"

—**Joyce Blackmere**, Director of Sales, The Dan Gemus Team

"Highly recommended!

This is a must read for team leaders, team members, or anyone thinking of starting or joining a team. Kathleen's no nonsense, real life advice is exactly what the real estate world needs right now."

—**Bill Madder**, CEO Saskatchewan Realtors Association

"Literally, can change your life course!

Easy to read, profound truths and extraordinary mix of real life and proven results. You'll feel the pull to experience 1% LIFE!!!"

—**Doug Schneider**, Lead Pastor, The Embassy Church

"Makes you remember what is important in life!

Very insightful and inspiring. Makes you realize that if you implement the right systems in your business, you can truly enjoy the life that has been afforded by all of your hard work. Well received."

—**Shannon Smith**, Lead Conversion Specialist,
Director of Sales/Coaching

"Fantastic Read!

The way Kathleen draws on her own life experiences, and how she overcame and dominated over obstacles and challenges was incredibly inspiring. I highly recommend this book for anyone looking for ways to improve at work, at home, and at life."

—**Donna Murdock**, Nuclear Engineer

"An Absolute Must Read!

This is an absolute must read for anyone looking to take control of their business and live life to the fullest. The content is eye-opening, insightful and extremely valuable. Thoroughly enjoyed the read!"

—**Stacey Green**, Director of Operations

THE
TOP
1% LIFE

Shift From Chaos to Calm
in Your Business & Life

KATHLEEN BLACK

NEW YORK

LONDON • NASHVILLE • MELBOURNE • VANCOUVER

THE TOP 1% LIFE
Shift From Chaos to Calm in Your Business & Life

Published in New York, New York, by Morgan James Publishing in partnership with Difference Press. Morgan James is a trademark of Morgan James, LLC. www.MorganJamesPublishing.com

ISBN 978-1-63195-098-8 paperback
ISBN 978-1-63195-099-5 eBook
ISBN 978-1-63195-100-8 audio
Library of Congress Control Number: 2020906875

Cover Design Concept:
Nakita Duncan

Cover Design:
Megan Whitley,Creative Ninja Designs
megan@creativeninjadesigns.com

Editor:
Nkechi Obi

Book Coaching:
The Author Incubator

Morgan James is a proud partner of Habitat for Humanity Peninsula and Greater Williamsburg. Partners in building since 2006.

Get involved today! Visit
www.MorganJamesBuilds.com

For my children, Ethan and Ella, who made bending time worthwhile, put up with my endless ideas, and were always being each other's support team. I love you the most forever.

For my team. Without you, getting epic stuff done would not exist. You are absolutely the best and make everything I had to do to get to this team worth it. You amaze me. I love you all.

This is just the beginning.

TABLE OF CONTENTS

Introduction

EXPANSION, COURAGE, REBELLION AND THE AUDACITY TO CHANGE

I have always been fascinated by expansion. Even as a young girl, I would marvel at the stories of those who could, and would, change the world. I don't think any of that fascination was by accident because later it led me to a hyper curiosity about people like you. People who could bend the world in their favour, create new realities, and use their time, energy, money, and focused on things of the highest importance to them. Whether it is Olympians, entrepreneurs, professional athletes, freedom fighters, writers, or those in sales, I always marvel at the audacity of those who dare to build in their best interest and found that their best interest also aligns with how they can be of highest service in this world.

I read story after story of those on a mission to live a top life and sought clarity and alignment to achieve their version of life, and they almost always felt they had carved that life against the grain. I believe a lot of us have a drive to expand and evolve. Because you have this book in your hands, or playing in your ear, I believe you also have a drive to expand and evolve. You are seeking expansion, as well. It may look like clarity, organization, and help to get you your time back, or it might allow you to leverage and grow your business. No matter what, the path to those goals lies in a clear, aligned, and ever-expanding leader.

You do not get the life you want by waiting for it to come to you, you get it by strengthening your clarity; when you do that, you will see that you now have the tools and systems from this book to achieve your goals. You can have the life of your dreams and an expanding business as long as you allow yourself the strength to act in order to build it. I believe that at our cores, we all live for expansion, evolution, growth, truth, service, and love. Expansion appears in many different ways, goals, faces, challenges, and lessons.

At some point I bet you felt unsettled. I know I did. You just knew something was off. Maybe it was a whisper, a feeling of overwhelming chaos, or an abrupt circumstance that screamed for your attention. We all get the call to expand, but not everyone chooses to listen. The trouble with ceasing to hear the whispers of your life, is that they become drowned out with your avoidance. A headache ongoing for years dulled by the ever-increasing amounts of Advil ceases to be as noticeable or painful, even if it is lovingly trying to get your attention about an issue in your brain. We so often confuse love and service as only soft or comforting, but the truths whispered in highest service to the expansion of our lives can be excruciatingly painful. These events can stop us in our tracks and cause us to question who we are and what we want. At worst, they cause us to question if we are worthy, capable, or meant to build the life we desire.

I have heard these wake-up calls so often, several times over, that now I am at home with the whispers, no longer needing to guard myself when change knocks at my doorstep. You don't fight as much when you know that change will happen regardless of how much you fight it. The only area of choice and focus is if you will choose to grow now that you have this gift of change, or will you fight to avoid the very calls sent to help you awaken and expand?

There are many ways to avoid your call to expand and evolve. I like to think of this call to expand and evolve as a personal and peaceful call to internally arm yourself. This is your call to fight for your own authentic voice, gifts, and truths. You can ignore this call when you stay too busy, but in the silence in those eye of the storm moments, you choose either to hear, listen, and act or to hear and ignore. Those moments define us all.

When we choose to arm ourselves, we choose the plight of our own personal warriors standing on guard of our true selves. It is a fight to honour, support, protect, and treasure the path of expansion within ourselves. It is in the resistance to the "weak mind", the one that tells us we can't, we shouldn't, we aren't strong enough, and we aren't brave enough that we win the battle. In ignoring the *very* loud roar of a world that wants to know "who the hell do you think you are," that we guard our paths to move forward. This is where the audacious choose to rebel and change. We are not rebelling against the world, but against a diminished, outdated, muted version of ourselves.

We can rebel against who we were yesterday. We all have the audacity to change if we choose to. First, we have to have the clarity to want to make changes, and the laser focus on where we are going.

When we look to take our time and life back, we demand to hold the reigns of the choices and circumstances that will build what we will call the destiny of our lives. When we pick up our arms, we hold the weapons to honour, protect, and nurture what is best in us from everything that is untrue and would hold us back. The majority of these lies about our lack of capability and resistance to expand life are only within ourselves. These limitations are not true in the real world.

A fearful mind will not trust its guide. To move and change in your business you must first step away from fear, into choice and possibility, and then you will have the ability to harness your business expansion toward a Top 1% Life.

I share this because any great book journey requires a brave, confident heart. You and I are about to go on a journey back in time. We will go back to the place where I started to help entrepreneurs, like you, accept their call to arms, stand strong in the chaos of their lives, and face the storm with a realization of who they were and what they could accomplish and with the clarity to take action. They had to stand in who they were before they could see and act on where they were going.

This book is a bridge back to the beginning of coaching, supporting, and choosing to build a life that focusses on working to power up people and support leaders, like you, opposed to building a life that focuses solely on serving expansion in myself.

I used to lie on the floor of my bathtub with the shower on as a child. I would turn the water to cold to envision children without proper food or shelter. I can't explain why I did this, aside from wanting to not only envision their pain and struggle but also to feel some small taste immersion. I wanted to sample that state of pain and despair so I could envision overcoming it. I would write endless essays, stories, and poems on the rights of children, and the need to fill this missing voice and void of the child.

Of course, it makes sense that I would write of rights betrayed and focus on limitations because I was fascinated by growth and expansion. I wanted to be free to face challenges, to learn, and grow. I wanted to eliminate the ceilings I perceived in the way of freedom, because I mistakenly thought only when I removed the ceilings could I be free to plant the seeds of my future. I was wrong.

I spent over half of my life educating myself about bias, rights, privilege, and discrimination in order to understand power in the context of voice, control, force, power, and privilege. I spent so much time focused on the things that limited me that I dulled my ability to hear my call to arms, to see myself as the warrior, and to honour my real weapons or my ability to walk away from anyone who I perceived to hold power over me. When I finally realized that the odds may have been against me but I was no statistic, victim, or any other label which may have prevented my growth, I also realized that I was strong and could plant, cultivate, and harvest the seeds of my future. I choose to spend the rest of my life nurturing that expansion into leadership, with not only myself, but with everyone around me who will listen and accept the call in themselves.

It's why I started working with good people who are very successful, but need time, energy, and health. Frankly, they need a life, and I can say that because everyone who knows me, knows sometimes I need time for a life too!

These people did not start out with mega teams. They were not teams at all. We built step by step together. Some grew to mega team status, and others just wanted enough help to be organized and take their time back. Now I often work with mega teams, but I started by building them. We built with our clientele to bring our community into existence. We are still building.

This book is my bridge back to build with some of you. The stories are not identified by my clients' names, but they are similar to the stories we all know in the team space today, before admins, agents, or any help to expand with the overflowing opportunities we created. At the end of this book, I will invite you to continue our journey face to face, by attending a complimentary webinar as a gift to you, which is located on my thank you page on the last page of this book.

This journey is for people who are serious about getting strong in any of life's storms, knowing who you are, what you stand for, and that you are now ready to use this new found clarity and strength to harness methods to expand into a reality where you can thrive in business *and* live your personal version a Top 1% Life.

I have spent over 18,000 hours personally one on one with leaders at the heights of their industries who needed a change. In addition, my coaching teams have spent tens of thousands of hours supporting leaders with the same Ultimate Expansion Journey we will take together in this book.

Achieving what you truly want is not only quicker, and easier, with the support of a proven path, but it also requires a like-minded community around you. That community is a necessity for fulfilling your ultimate expansion. We are not simply who we are, we are the interpretation of our thoughts echoed back to us by those around us. We become what we surround ourselves with, so I highly encourage you to connect with others for a monthly book club, online community conversation, and to compare valuable takeaways that you have committed to take action on in your life. I have needed a team of like-minded people my whole life, so I built one, and I would like to invite you to join us at the end of this book.

I want you to know that when you accept your call to arms, you will become the warrior you need to be to make the changes you want. You will be able to build a business that is the natural progression of your clarity and choices. Until you choose to arm yourself, you will wait for the world to deliver you an ideal life, you will wait for the promotion, the change, and the acknowledgements that all lie externally outside of yourself. You will be waiting for a while if you choose that path – potentially forever. The world will not even know what you are waiting for because the world responds to who you decide and believe you are. The world cannot promote you. That power only lies in yourself.

Stop waiting for a promotion to your ideal life, and, instead, build it for yourself. You will have to do the work and fight for it. I am writing this book because I am addicted to leverage as a natural by-product of my fascination with expansion. My niche lives in powerhouse sales teams, and I am excited to arm you with the experience and path of thousands before you in building your very own Top 1% Life.

Chapter 1

IN THE EYE OF THE STORM

R emember that time you hustled to make it to your family dinner on time? Usually, you're late or miss dinner altogether, but you were determined to make it to this one. You hustled to get there only to be glued to your phone, constantly excusing yourself for calls, emails, texts, and personal messages. The frustration was mounting for everyone. You couldn't help but feel the shame of a business that was so "successful" it was out of control.

It is hard to pinpoint the exact moment when things moved from working so hard to build your business, to making enough to support your family, to getting to a place where you just want a break. How does it shift so quickly?

I remember meeting with clients on New Year's Day in a snowstorm. It was my first year in the business. Mark and Nancy really needed a place to live. They were desperate, scared, and worried. They had a family and house to look after. They had little children and were going into a brand-new year that should have been full of what all New Year's days should hold: hope, excitement, and anticipation for the beautiful gifts a fresh start would bring. Instead, they were paralyzed with fear, and I was feeling the pressure. They were given very little notice to leave the rental home they lived in for several years and were never confident enough to buy. They just got by financially with the rate of rent and family expenses. Now, they had no choice but to move, and without the resources to buy, they would once again succumb to a rental market where rates skyrocketed. They would now be further behind with less monthly cash flow.

Here I was, driving through streets void of cars or people, hoping their vehicle would make it through the snow, that we would find them a place to feel safe and rebuild; and that I could be enough to solve their problem, take care of them, and figure it all out. If this was year two in the business, I would not have been there. A single mother myself with two young children, I knew the pressure of having to make one minute into two. I knew how to get by with not quite enough, and my heart went out to these people. In year two, I was no longer the woman I was in year one. I built better boundaries. The world knew Mark and Nancy needed help, and the world brought them to me. In that first year, in that moment, I could help them. And I did.

I had this small window where I could help them rebuild, to feel safe, to move forward. And when I did, I completed a cycle that they did not even know existed. This time, I got to be the guide. Last time, I was the desperate one, needing but lacking a guide for myself. I never entertained the thought that I needed a guide, though. Why wish for gumballs without quarters? The desperate do not dream as much as they hustle. Dreaming requires time without urgency or a calm in a storm when you have finally broken from carrying all this world has asked of you. A break in time or a break in spirit—that is where dreaming lives. While some dream of gumballs, we collect change on the floor. Magically, eventually, we have quarters.

I was relieved to end the cycle I knew so well. Relieved that I got to give back. That is what I believe we were all brought into this world to do. We have moments and experiences where things are taken from us. Sometimes, the cruelest experiences can be out of your control, and life will rip your most delicate gifts from your hands. The loss of time, people, and circumstances carved my life. I have a feeling loss carves the best of us, and it carved the best of my clients that day.

I did help them find a lease, and once we had a break from the urgency of the situation, I connected them with the resources to build the dream of owning a home of their own. I so wanted them to have the power to choose, to carve out the life that was just beyond the horizon waiting for them. I so wanted them to know that they were worthy and capable. That they, too, could morph from this experience into people who cast a light for others. A gift they gave me.

A few years later, I would find out that Mark was sick. He was battling cancer and had to step away from his job and income. I would discover later that they saw the decision to lease as a saving grace as they could not bear to find a home only to lose it and have to walk away. Nancy shared the heavyweight of their lives before the illness. She shared the tight rope that was the journey of keeping a broken marriage together to house their children without the means to do so on their own, apart from each other. Nancy would eventually leave Mark after he was well, back to work, and they were on their feet again. She rebuilt in the end. She eventually even bought a home. She caught the same strength to make big changes at a rare, quiet moment. She told me that she had to make a leap exactly when she knew she was strong enough to go. Leaving was a glimpse, a fraction of a second when her mind, body, and soul found resolve, and she took that moment of calm, and she jumped. It was the perfect timing for a change. She clawed her way back onto her feet and she found a way to get out of debt, so she would have enough to make her own choices.

I did not tell Nancy how much we had in common. I was a successful real estate agent. I made more money than I ever made before. I helped forty-five people buy and sell homes in my first year in real estate. I signed thirteen beautiful people to work with me exclusively as buyers in my first month in the business. But just months before I helped Nancy, I had a dirty little secret. I was showing up at the office. I was helping my clients. I never missed a meeting or an appointment. But I was not living in my own home anymore.

I was sharing a room in my mother's and stepfather's home with my two children. I would answer ad calls in the hallway, feed my children McDonald's on the go, and buy a small toddler bed to sit on the floor beside me when Children's Aid Society (CAS) said it was too dangerous to let my 2.5-year-old daughter who nursed for over two years and co-slept with ease, sleep in bed with my son and me. I still resent that part. CAS stayed on me and kept my file open for two years as I desperately tried to navigate the path out of marriage into separation and, after five long years, finally, a divorce. But they stayed on to support me. They knew I needed someone to help me decipher what was happening. How do you go from building a small empire, with retirement in sight within ten years, being dubbed the "no money miracle" of investment acquisition, leaning into sweat equity with every fiber of your being, to frozen accounts, locked doors, and restraining orders?

You force yourself to continue despite the storm.

This situation got me back into my family home for now. It allowed me to find some sense of normalcy while I ramped up my energy into my real estate business. I would be the breadwinner now. There was no financial support. There was no help.

Nancy's situation happened months later. Helping them brought up my own sense of protection for my children and family.

It all felt too familiar. So, I moved myself. With two weeks' notice, we packed our home, found a rental, and moved into a house.

Why do we lean so hard into building successful businesses? Because we know life happens, and we want to be prepared. We want to be more than prepared for that next surprise around the corner. We get stuck in the feeling of needing to build far beyond the point of financial security. So, we answer the call. We reply to the email. We miss the birthday party. We sit in the living room during holidays while our minds sit far away in the office. We hope no one notices, and if they do notice, we hope they understand. We hope they can see the sacrifices to feel safe, capable, and well-resourced. We hope they know we are well-intentioned in never wanting them to go through what we did, ever again.

So, it makes sense that we fail to notice the shift. It makes sense that we are so conditioned to jump and react, to fear the day we do not hear the phone ringing or have a client that needs us, leaving us to sit in mental scarcity without noticing the world shifted around us.

We fail to notice the bank accounts growing, the clients referring, and the time sliding away from us. We miss the moments when we dreamed of making this much. No champagne. No celebration. We were naive when we set those goals, naive to think this would be enough to risk pulling back or slowing down.

So, we forge on. We set new goals that we never acknowledge achieving and consistently feel it is all so very short of what we need, what we want, what we expected. We tell ourselves we still do not have enough—we still are not enough to fight the dragons if they were to ever show their faces again. So, we save more, do more, and give more. We beat the odds, we laugh in the face of statistics, and we sit in glass houses wishing they were concrete. We sit wishing our houses were dragon-proof while simultaneously believing we are fighting the dragon just one more call, one more client, and one more paycheck at a time.

The eye of the storm is when you have moments of clarity that provide windows into how to act in life and business. When you feel pressured for answers, the clarity that you have will give you a brief moment to change. Those moments change your life. They are a brief glimpse into what could be despite the noise. They are portals to the future. If you get one, take it.

Chapter 2

LEADERSHIP BY FIRE

It was December 25th, 2015, and I just said goodbye to my children as they left for some holiday time with their dad. I looked around my empty house, the unwrapped presents, the Christmas tree, and the remnants of chocolate wrappers. All I could see, taste, smell, and feel were silence. The silence started to creep into a crack that would become an end, a surrender to the recent months of unravelling. Unravelling sounds calm and beautiful. But, it wasn't. That final surrender, and what resulted, became the catalyst for some of the best work of my life as well as the quickest business growth.

About five years prior, around 2010, I was ecstatic to start running the first team-specific coaching company for real estate in Canada. I was thrilled at the new challenge and opportunity. Eighteen months into the launch of the new company, I became director of coaching. With issues in two key areas, content and retention, I decided to pull back and strengthen both areas before launching any new growth initiatives. This was a risky move because the company was struggling. Cash flow is king, but client experience is queen, and if I know one thing about sales, it is that people sell what they believe in, both to potential clients and to themselves.

I wanted a company that I, our coaching team, and sales team believed in, and I insisted on a company our clients could believe in. This meant eighteen months of strict content creation and improvement before adding any additional programs, events, or new projects. Luckily, as a single mom selling over sixty houses a year, I knew all about refining systems and the efficiency and mindset needed to excel.

Our sales team manager would often ask me how I sold as many homes as our top producers in half the work hours. Now, I was selling the same plus coaching and running the coaching team. This took a massive amount of patience for me. I had so many dreams and visions for the company. I instantly devoted my foreseeable business future to leading the coaching team. I envisioned a point where I would only coach and no longer sell. I loved helping others to grow and succeed.

Over time, my goal shifted to being the head of all clients. Our mission was to carve the path ahead of our top producing teams to create an ever-increasing cohesive business, building systems to the top that others could easily follow while keeping our top teams thriving. It had to be efficient, profitable, deliver results, and make life better for our clients' teams, clients, and leaders. We sought to elevate the team platform as the ultimate destination for a new agent, struggling agent, or well-established agent who was sick of doing it all to excel.

These teams started working with me at twenty-five resale deals exceeding 550 units annually. What was unique about this was the level of coaching and training. We sought to transfer knowledge, coach implementation, and maintain what we had built as we scaled into further growth. We were not looking for one-off success stories. It had to be real, consistent, and true. We built with our top clients step-by-step. We effectively reduced the cost of research and testing by 90% or altogether in some areas. We found a massive edge and even started to exceed our own internal best in class baselines. Teams at 300k Gross Commission Income (GCI) exceeded 1 million dollars GCI. Our coaching team mastered the compensation structure, allowing one of our clients to scale to over 1,000 homes sold a year.

The results were easy to see. When most companies were focused on 5 to 10% increases for their coaching clients per year, we sought best-in-class for our clients. We celebrated the doubling of units and gross earnings for clients every year. 10X and 20X business growth became a reality for our network, meaning we grew the businesses to ten and twenty times the size of the business compared to when we first started working with them. Over time, our results became difficult for the real estate industry to relate to and understand.

I always knew that the team concept was its own niche in any sales industry used to celebrating solo producers, but I never realized how vastly different the mentality and the results would be from those living in the team reality. We created our own events and stages when the industry would not welcome us on theirs, and largely, this is still the case today.

Less than a year after accepting my role as director of coaching, things changed again. I was needed as Director of Operations. Now, this title is misleading. Director of Operations was a culmination of Director of Coaching, Director of Marketing, Director of Finance, and Director of Operations all in one. The original Director of Coaching was let go and, as a result, I was getting my feet wet trying to run a whole company with no actual experience or training on running a business, let alone a business in the volatile and competitive coaching industry. Finally, I had the notion to ask to see the books. Now, how a company was able to get about $180k in debt in less than two years is beyond me. There was no line up of others looking to run the company, there was less than no money, and I was starting to understand that the weight of our rebound as a business fell on my shoulders.

In the middle of all of this, two of the three owners wanted out, were wanted out, or both. They each had various director roles, but none of them had all of them.

When we were rebuilding, I only focused on what it would take. I had no space to compare job descriptions, responsibilities, or contemplate the full weight of what I was taking on. If I failed to clean up this mess, it would be me to blame, and if I succeeded, it would not be my name taking that claim either. So, I was back picking up change on the ground, knowing I was relentless enough to find enough for a few quarters. The rest could wait.

My mentality was more like, "Run a business doing what I love? Sign me up!" I was not thinking about the debt or ridiculous amount of responsibilities and tasks. I was focused on the dream.

Taking a massive pay cut, I finally transitioned away from selling homes to continue to build content, support our clients, run national events, and keep it all in the black while we cleared debt.

I had the realization that I was now the company. I literally obtained 50% ownership with 100% decision-making as the two owners transitioned out. I saw the mess that came with multiple owners and wanted no part of it. If I was going to clear the full amount of debt, including the 50% I now owned, and find a way out to where we could grow, I needed to move fast, straight, and reduce sideline interference.

I cleared the debt. We built phenomenal businesses with our clients where their growth was evident and a direct reflection of the new approach of the company. But then my silent partner suddenly grew less silent.

We agreed upfront that I was to earn a "fairer" income once the debt was cleared, the company was on its feet again, and I could forge ahead with my dreams for expansion, being rewarded as we grew. But suddenly, he felt we should go in a different direction. That I should take a pay cut, again, and automate the company so it was more plug and play. I made offer after offer to buy him out, to license the content I already technically owned, and come to some agreement so we could get back to what we should have been doing all along: helping people build their dream business and life.

No offers were countered, and on October 1st, 2015, I arrived at locked doors. I quickly was informed that my clients were told I was fired. Now, anyone who knows about business understands the impossibility of this. I was a 50% owner who was not consulted in firing the CEO, who held 100% decision-making power, and that person, the CEO in question, happened to be me.

None of the legal issues changed the immediate reality that I was scared and thought I lost everything I worked for. Every missed night of my children's sporting or school events, every missed meal, all the financial sacrifices were for nothing.

How could I look my children in the face? How could I stand tall or proud? I was tricked. Despite the high odds of being screwed, this was a fire sale I had to jump on. Something in me waged the internal war with risk and knew that I was at a disadvantage, but the possibility of building something great and the experience of running my own company was impossible to turn down.

We had sent all ownership agreements to the lawyer long ago, signed by both me and the other silent partner. The ownership was all done, but we still spent months negotiating the prior owner out of the business—a business I needed to run with clients to support. Because of this we had delayed going to the lawyer to officially update the corporate documents.

My life went spinning out of control. I was terrified. The bank delivered old ownership documents without our updated agreements and already froze the accounts. I was enraged, sad, and felt deeply betrayed. I play fair, and this situation did not have an ounce of fair to its name.

To say I was depressed would be a lie. I was too shocked to be depressed. It would come out that the other owner thought I did not have the resources to fight him. He banked on my fear and need to support my children. He banked on me not having the guts or courage to stand up for myself. I was not paid that month as I often would pay our team first, ensuring we had the funds for them first.

My lawyer had to escalate to other specialized lawyers, as "they just don't see this type of thing. It makes no sense to do this." It was all taking so much time.

I was lucky to have a little voice that changed it all. A guide appeared this time with an important message. It said, "If you believe in it, and it is right, you do not need to hide or cower. You bank everything you have on it. You bet your house on it and get the resources you need to make this right." It was this voice combined with a single self-empowering question, "What would you guide your clients to do in a similar situation?" that convinced me, without a doubt, I would stand for my clients and fight beside them. Now, I had to do the same for myself.

Finally, I made it in front of a judge and then to mediation. I literally had to bet my house on hiring that lawyer, paying over $800 an hour for my lawyer alone, day after day and week after week went. Having no resolve was terrifying. I was exhausted. The legal bill was mounting. Finally, we got clear direction from our mediating judge that the ownership agreement may not be in the corporate documents, but there was not a judge in the country that would overturn our ownership agreement or turn a blind eye to the fact that I was running the company as the owner for years.

The tides changed. I accepted an offer to sell my shares, and in an unbelievable change of fate, I also got to keep half of our clients. Both of us were to retain ownership of all intellectual content with the ability to legally start and promote a new company as of December 1st, 2015. The final share exchange and payout would happen January 15th, 2016.

December 1st, I was able to bill in my own name. I had clients who took a chance on me, but I had no income for two months, a stack of expenses, and was still terrified. I was still in shock and, luckily, too terrified not to hit the ground running. Within three weeks, my coaching schedule was more than full. Within two months, I brought in another coach. He came in with two clients paying in packs of two or four hours and using them as needed over weeks or months. He was now full with ongoing clients and we sought to hire another coach within six months.

Upon opening Kathleen Black Coaching & Consulting in 2015, we earned 35% more in gross income in our first full operational year followed by approximately 84% more in our second operating year over the 2015 gross income of my previous company. I went from fear and desperation to quickly scaling a company.

Your Own Face of Leadership

Most of us know all about unravelling. We went through the blunt transitions that unpack our former lives and try to morph us at a lightning speed into the new version of ourselves now needed by the present and future world.

I stood with clients during times of unravelling. I watched as changing aspects, often out of their control, impacted their lives, businesses, and even their sense of self in a way that seemed to cripple them with anxiety, fear, embarrassment, self-judgement, and the associated stress from the whole experience. From losing team members, to health issues, to divorce, to teenagers, to having to let people go, so many aspects of life and business can unravel you and leave you questioning your next move. I also watched clients rebuild better, stronger, and faster using the power that comes from pain properly harnessed. Most leaders are said to rise from the ashes. These leaders face the mirror of truth in crisis. They decide to carve their own face of leadership in the place they previously and recklessly left for the world to define. They decided who they were and what they would and would not stand for.

I know what it feels like to build a business from nothing, the burn when a team member leaves, the shock when you find out someone is sabotaging your business. The deep feeling of violation when someone you supported steals from you or lies to you. The feeling when people leave and use your content, when you find out you were lied to, locked out, and even when others take credit for your work. I know what it feels like, and I know the hardest part is facing it all and moving forward. Because the world needs strong business leaders like you, who are true and spread a different message.

I stood in these difficult spaces as I built seven-figure companies with countless clients, and as I did the same for myself. I struggled with exactly the best way to transfer what worked for me to my team. I had unbelievably high expectations and little room for lowering them. I had to up my game knowing we would take a hit as a business to make those changes. And I have had to stand for the truth, more than once despite, massive costs. Why did I make the changes anyway? Because a company that runs without an abundance mentality and without aligned guiding principles is doomed to fail. You can take a 75, 50, or 20% hit now or risk losing it all later. I stand in hard decisions because if I don't, who will? I believe that by standing in hard decisions, I discover exactly who else will. You will, our clients will, and everyone impacted by all of your hard decisions will have the courage to make them too. We live what we see. Doing the hard things right matters.

It is not *if* these difficult things will happen. It is *when* difficult obstacles present themselves in your business. And when these difficult things happen in business that challenge your vision, heart, and soul, I want you to know others went through this, how to keep going, and when to limit your time energy and resources so small acts do not cost you big in the long run.

Sure, it's just business, but it feels personal when that business involves people who you helped and the resources sacrificed to build that business. I built my business to systematically reduce the odds of anything negative ever repeating that could compromise my team, clients, or ability to be of service in this world. I also built hundreds of teams and the businesses of thousands of agents and helped them to avoid ever hitting the common pitfalls. If the acts of one sabotage the true gift of helping and serving others on a local or global scale, it is costing us all. We need to build our businesses to protect the people we serve, and in your business, that is you and your team.

Some things require a burn. Some lessons only happen when the world gets hot enough to forge the lesson in your skin. Then, you get to work building better, and ensuring the small acts of one person never cost you or your team the whole.

Chapter 3

HOW DO I GET MY TIME BACK?

Myth: *Teams take too much time and money to develop.*

Truth: The function of a team is to provide more time and money with less expense and effort put in by the team leader. In fact, when done properly, effectively, and systematically, creating and running a team is highly profitable and frees up time for all team members, including you.

That admin support you hired took more of your time than your clients. I hear this reality every day from people who have tried to get help. Our team hears this hundreds of times a week. Hiring her added to your to-do list because you were walking an uphill battle before you started.

Trying to hire, build a job description, the systems and tasks associated with that job description, and train, all at once is basically impossible. People are told, every day, hiring support is the answer, and it is when you are prepared.

The buyer's agent needs you constantly because he wants you to be happy. He wants the clients to be happy. He wants to know how to win, how to do a good job, and what to avoid, but lacks the deliberate strategy and clarity that duplication of values and standards requires of your team's business. You're always trying to keep deals together. You are busy enough. Eventually, if you have tried to hire, you may have decided that it seemed easier to just do it on your own, but now what?

It is true that it may be easier to run your business on your own in the short-term. Servicing clients yourself in your custom way is quicker than creating the tasks, job description, hiring, and training it takes to expand your team. But what happens to that same time trade-off after one, two, or three years—heck, even three months?

Just for fun, write a list of all the tasks that a support position could do for you. Now, write how long each of those tasks takes you per week. Now, add them up. You can now compare how many weeks of you personally doing those tasks it would take you to do it to equal the amount of time you are estimating it will take to hire, which will likely include creating the task list (which we just started), creating the job description, interviewing, and training. Your hiring process should be no more than two to three weeks at most. Beyond that, the amount of time to accomplish those tasks on your own becomes indefinite.

Over and above the time factor or the money factor, the reality is that doing it on your own is not going to help you make it home for dinner on time. If you want time to spend your nights and weekends with your children, spouse, and loved ones, you are going to need someone to help with the business. Most sales and service industries do not shut down in the evenings or on the weekends. There is more demand than ever for after-hours options in all industries. Do you expect timely answers when you need them from a lawyer, doctor, accountant, or when you need to make a business decision? Your clients feel the same way about wanting access to your level of wisdom and resources when they need them.

While you could develop a business model around the nine-to-five workweek, you will have some clients deciding to go elsewhere, which will be an overall hit to business volume. For most of us, this is not a realistic solution. We want to elevate client experience, not reduce it.

You will need help that actually makes a difference for your business and helps get your business organized and self-sufficient so everything doesn't depend on you anymore. This relief will free up time and energy to do more of what you love and do best. The ability to do more of what you love, when done right, will increase your overall business earnings even after you bring in and pay support staff. Am I saying you will do less and make more? Yes, that is exactly what I am saying.

To have the time to confidently hire, and expand, and do less, you will need to get yourself to a place where you stop being on call 24/7. After you get some help, you will be close to taking an actual vacation—without your phone. The truth is that your business will likely be ready for you to take a vacation without your phone before you will be. You won't need to be there for everything that comes up. You need to be able to let some things wait, condition your clients on when they can expect to hear from you, and free up your time so you can work on what is of the greatest importance that hour or day.

Right now, the ability to get some time back, get organized, and find some help you can rely on is of greatest importance. This is your eye of the storm. This is your moment to get the resources you need to step into a future version of you that already has more time, meals with your family, a life away from your phone, an organized office, and a business that does not rely on you every second of the day. This future version of you exists. All you must do is access the resources while they are available to you.

I am your guide on this journey to your future self and future business. I will take you through the steps to building this new reality sequentially. Don't bother jumping ahead steps or chapters as this journey builds upon each step as we go. For example, you don't want to use your current eyes to read the chapter on "No More Babysitting." Your current eyes created the business you have now. We love those eyes. They got you here, but, point-blank, they are not the eyes that will get you the time and life you want in the future.

Together, I will help you expand on how you see your business, yourself, and your role in that business. You will carve out what you love to do most, take away what you dislike doing, and work to create the ultimate momentum maker: leverage.

Once you know what you love and how you will step into your next phase of leadership, we will carve out your unique values, allowing for the space and training to attract others to help you create these values and believe in them alongside you to serve your clients. This is the key to leverage that so many business owners miss. It is not enough to get more done or to get more done without needing you. The key to successful leverage is to elevate the end experience or product for everyone involved. We want to have a better experience and a more successful outcome for you, your team, and your clients. That is what leverage is all about. It is the ultimate unfair advantage!

Once you are ready to leverage your time, you will need some help. That means a process is needed to hire, recruit, and train. You will need to know how to build your business and how to thrive by creating a performance environment. A performance environment is part of the sales-speak that is rarely defined and often turns into lingo used by the coaching industry. Although rarely explained, performance environments do exist, and they are a make-or-break for your business. So, instead of just talking like you know what a performance environment is, you are going to carve out the exact ingredients you will need to build one. I will explain why you can hire someone of average talent and watch them kick butt in a performance environment compared to someone with exceptional talent who will struggle.

KBCC Ultimate Expansion Strategy

The following steps in the Kathleen Black Coaching & Consulting Inc. (KBCC) Ultimate Expansion Strategy will allow you to get help faster while avoiding common mistakes, which leave most leaders back at the beginning doing it all themselves. Expansion does not have to be painful, although it does have to be focused and brave. These steps will walk you through a tried, tested, and true process to safeguard your role, your time, your client experience, and your business as you grow.

Step 1: Bullseye! That is the Business I Want!

In this step, you will gain clarity before action and know exactly what you want and why to act with confidence.

Step 2: The Mindset Matrix to Stunningly Successful

You will learn the perspective of successful business owners to build with new eyes and go from overworked, under-achieving solopreneur to stunningly successful business owner.

Step 3: Addicted to Leverage: The GENIUS Method

Know your strengths and weaknesses as a leader. This step will allow you to delegate away tasks that cost you time and money in your business to capable team members. You will then have more time to focus on what you love, earn more money, and have more time overall.

Step 4: Your Values, Your Standards, Your Reputation, Done Your Way

In this step, I will show you how you can offer a better service and a superior result to clients by expanding your team and doing less yourself.

Step 5: Stop Babysitting! Get Help Without Hiring Sales Agents

In this step, I will show you how a hiring and recruitment system will save you time, money, and frustration. You will learn exactly what you have to offer to a potential recruit or hire and to stop trying to recreate the wheel by implementing a proven system instead.

Step 6: Avoiding Common and Costly Mistakes

In this step, you will discover the best plan for you to expand by following a tried, tested, and true path that saves you time, money, and frustration. Discover the power of "Model the Best: Forget the Rest" in your business.

Step 6: How to Create Performance Culture

In this step, you will learn the key ingredients in a performance culture, so you can structure your business to hold accountability for results and excel with a skilled sales team. You will also explore your ROI when you build a well-performing team and understand when to limit resources if a team member is not performing.

Step 7: Built to Win: Team Synergy

The world is changing. You are not alone in feeling this transition. The need to change is not limited to your business. This expansion is part of a vital shift toward greater professionalism and consulting and is demanded by consumers from the sales industry globally. Elevating your business means contributing to the personal development of your team, community, country, and the world.

The steps outlined above will make sense and provide you with a clear path for you to get the help you need and want. Even with such a clear strategy, it will be tempting to do some things differently. Every business owner has their unique approach, which we want to nurture. However, you do not want to get stuck in avoidable and common mistakes. The common mistakes are almost always the ones that we think make genuine good sense and are unique to us. Ninety-nine% of the time, the common mistakes are really common, and they pop up as genius ideas to avoid doing what we need to do to build a business people will stay in, thrive in, and love.

Today is the day to leave the "overworked underachiever" concept behind. You outgrew the long hours, the costs to your personal life, the effects on your health, and you might even realize that you outgrew the cost of delivering less than your best work to the world. No more diluting your gifts, your time, or your life.

You watched others build a stunningly successful life, and now it's time for you to do the same with the Ultimate Expansion Strategy leading the way.

Chapter 4

BULLSEYE! THAT IS
THE BUSINESS I WANT!

I still remember the first "SCREW THIS" moment I ever had. I had to be fed up enough to carve a line in the sand. My lines look more like systems with steps, agreements, and expectations, but a line no less.

I was struggling to sell so many homes, take care of my children, go to the gym, keep my energy up, avoid feeling sorry for myself, and deal with the massive stress of a very messy and difficult separation. Imagine a marriage and all the emotions that come with that, plus the business of multiple investment properties, one as a silent partner in my ex-husband's name, and a matrimonial home where I was not an official on title owner. Fun times all around.

As I hustled to get work done, I was criticized for feeding my children McDonald's. It did not matter that I cooked ninety-five% of every meal and every huge family dinner from scratch until then. The hours upon hours with icing tips making cartoon character birthday cakes were all forgotten.

My son made a simple comment. He mentioned that one of his grandmothers said I should be cleaning his room and doing his laundry for him. He also seemed to be of the new opinion that I did not need to make as much money as I was and could afford to work less. That, suddenly, I was choosing to spend less time with him. I don't know why that was the moment, or what divine intervention was being sent from above to shake me out of the senseless notion that I could be and have it all, but that was a moment where I finally got clarity and drew a line in the sand.

When I worked, I was told I worked too much and should be with my children.

When I was with my children, I was told my house needs my attention. Don't you have laundry to do and rooms to clean?

When I considered a cleaning lady, I was lazy.

When I tried to make amends to save my marriage, I was crazy.

Trust me, the list goes on, and I do not think this list is unique to me.

So, the moment happened, and with crystal clear clarity, I knew. I could never win. Not for a single second. I could never be enough of a woman, mother, realtor, coach, CEO, wife, partner, friend, sister, or daughter to make this world happy.

The same people that would say I worked too much would be the same ones to claim I should get off my butt and work if I stayed home, worked part-time, or needed social assistance.

Enough was enough. I needed to get clear on who I was, what I stood for, and where I was going to choose to put my time, money, and attention. I was in a lose-lose scenario that was causing so much stress and anxiety, it was costing me even more time and money.

The thing is that everyone meant well. They were all trying to help me to lead my best life. The trouble was that they were using their recipe for how to do life right and applying it to me. It was not my recipe, but I did not really know what my recipe was, which meant I was open and susceptible to the fierce inner and outer criticism that comes from second-guessing yourself.

The hardest part I had to grapple with on the journey to knowing my personal recipe for how I wanted to do life was this: What if they are right?

What if I am a bad mom, wife, friend? Until I could get clarity on what was really happening, the comments would get under my skin, and they stung uncontrollably. They hurt. At times, they sent me spinning out of control. I just could not get a strong grip on the reality of why people were being so ruthless in their expectations of me compared to that of themselves.

Terrified that what they were saying was true, I had to break out of it. Why would anything someone else said bother me if I did not find some merit in it? If I did not see any truth, then why should it matter?

This was a massive breakthrough. I was feeding the dragon. I was dangling treats of dripping, bloody meat that were small pieces of my heart. Why? Because I wanted someone else to see me. I wanted them to know and understand how hard I was trying and how much it all really hurt, but I could not communicate that yet. I was too busy being busy. I was too committed to proving them wrong and doing it on my own.

Just after leaving my matrimonial home, I finally got some relief when I set a sales goal: that if I sold enough, I would get help with cleaning. I was crystal clear about the current losing equation. Clean the house and have very little quality time with the kids. Don't clean the house and you are lazy. Well, I was not going to win in either of those scenarios, so I hit my goal and hired someone to clean bi-weekly. The relief was off the charts. I loved the feeling of a clean home among the demands of business and life, and I loved the way my focus aligned with my business and children in new ways. I had more time to think, connect, and feel joy. My time was worth more to me and to my bottom line financially.

Why do we hold back from paying others to do what supports them when it costs us the energy, time, and focus to lean into living the parts of this life we want to experience most?

I started to notice the same journey in my clients. They were trying to do it all. They were trying to convince themselves that they did not want business success, to be noticed by the world, or to walk across that stage to be recognized for the results of their work. I have clients who struggle to communicate their want to be home and their extreme guilt when they are away from their family while in busy sales environments wanting the souls of their sales partners to live, breathe, eat, pray, love, and dream of sales success alone.

I do not believe in balance. I never have. I never had balance and never really reached for it. It is unattainable, and just plain boring vanilla that makes me feel like I am in a school assembly with someone saying crisscross apple sauce, be quiet, play nice, and smile, you look so much prettier that way. Nope. I still feel uncomfortable at my children's school assemblies to this day. I wait for someone to get me in trouble, take away my phone, and tell me I am sitting in someone else's seat. True story to this day.

As Robin Sharma, a top leadership expert, instilled in me that top performers have on-seasons and they have off-seasons. I am not here to be average, and if you are reading this book, I doubt you are either. My father always said, "Average is very Average." I went through about twenty versions of what that quote means. Every time I approach it, I am a new woman, and, therefore, it is not the same quote. As Heraclitus, the Greek philosopher, said, "No man ever steps in the same river twice, for it's not the same river and he's not the same man." That is exactly how I feel about average being very average and everything else we learn. The deeper we go, the deeper we get.

What I do know is that average is a marker, a goal, a set point that anyone can set for themselves. This setpoint is safe, absorbed by the masses, and largely achievable. There is a lot of people living average for many different reasons. Some of those reasons we will discuss together. Why? Because average does not build a business that gives you more time, more money, and a better-quality experience and service for your clients.

Balance does not build the business or life that you want! So, what does?

Clarity

You need to decide what you want without any self-judgement. You need to become an advocate for yourself so you can better advocate for your clients, so you can protect the voices of others in times of joy and in times of pain. You will become an advocate for your team, and eventually for the future team member who will be joining your business very soon.

You do not build a business and stop. This is not a matter of completion. A business is a product of evolution and refinement into the ever-expanding nuance that is mastery. It never really ends, and you would not want it to. A business on standstill is a business with downhill momentum. New problems are good. The same problems are not so good. Your business will get to a point where it is bigger than you, but first, you need clarity on who you are and what you want, so you want to do what it takes. That is the key here. You will need to get to a place where your energy is high, and you want to do what it takes to get it done.

You want more time. You cannot imagine living this way two years from now. What about five or ten years from now? How does that vision feel? I am guessing not so good. So, what are you willing to do about it today and why?

In the end, I stopped giving my ear to those who did not support me. I got really picky about who I would ask for advice and whose unwarranted advice I would no longer take. I stopped caring about vanilla solutions in a world of rainbow ice cream. I prefer salted caramel gelato and a second scoop of pistachio served in Italy, thank you very much.

Back to the point. I had to make these changes this for a few reasons:

Someone Else's Recipe For Life Is Not Mine

Another word for this recipe is "values." We all have a unique combination of values. Essentially, this is the answer key for where we feel happy and fulfilled putting our time, energy, attention, and money. No one has the same test, so no one else has your answer key. Heck, most people do not even have their own answers figured out but have no problem trying to tell you what your recipe should be.

I Had to Stop Feeding the Dragon

My pain in trying to navigate a ridiculous number of tasks to do every day with very little help was sending the wrong signal to the world. Let's be honest, my signal was more like a distress flare on the side of the road after a head-on collision, but it was a signal all the same. What did it say? "Please see I am doing my best, tell me I am doing it right, tell me that I am good enough, and support me in trying to do better." Sounds transparent, honest, vulnerable, and all the good sweet stuff, right? *Wrong.* The world gave me more of what I was putting out there. I was communicating that I am misunderstanding myself when I needed to say, "Back off! I trust myself, I know my intentions are true, and I will do me (please and thank you!)."

The More I Opened Myself Up to a World, Wanting to Carve My According to its Most Immediate Wants and Needs, the Further I Got from My Authentic Self

I believe we are here to serve the world in a much higher frequency. Your purpose is unique to you. It was buried deep within you at birth. You have a unique path. Your job is to connect to and trust that path while being as gentle and honest to yourself and those around you as you go.

We Were Built Precisely for the Gifts, Journey, and Contribution We Are Meant to Make in This World

You were built to win, and so was I, but we are never going to win expecting other people's opinions, actions, and choices to reflect our worth. They do not decide our worth; we do.

I Needed to Be Open to Mentorship, Growth, and Positive Criticism

I wrote, year after year, that I was attracting precisely the people who would push me to my potential and see my capability to help others in this world. I read those words, and others, every day, sometimes multiple times a day, for years, and I called out for wisdom. We have to hold space for the voices who tell us we are screwing up. We need space for the voices who care enough to intervene when we are our own worst enemies and when we need a lesson because our choices in the next stage will be of a much more severe consequence.

When you have ill-intentioned voices in your ear, you lose the ability to hear the well-intentioned voices. They all just sound like criticism. Intention matters. Intention trumps and precedes action. I can prove this very simply: If your intention changes, so will your actions. Anyone acting out of an intention to serve and lead in the highest good to all will always come from a place of conscious thought, introspection, care, concern, abundance, and potentially, even from a place of humble apology. A voice that is ill-intentioned looks to hurt, judge, criticize, compare, or manipulate. An ill-intentioned voices live in scarcity and attract and recruit in scarcity. You can feel scarcity in your bones. Your body knows it before your mind sees and hears it. It is the place that lost hopes go to live in fear. Lost hope will not bring a voice of hope to others, but a hopeful voice can alleviate fear. The well-intentioned voices will help you elevate the fear, renew the hope, and proceed in faith. They will course correct and help you build and reinforce the banks of the river, which will protect the flow of who you decide you are.

I promise you, once you silence the voices with intentions to criticize, belittle, and use you, you will hear the voices of the ultimate privilege and gift this life will ever give you. Those voices are angels in my life. They are a privilege denied to most in this world. They are the voices that see you. They see your ability, and they did not even have to look. They want you to succeed, and they see and mirror your capabilities. Their voices will be painful and harsh at times, but they won't break you. Those voices will make you. Confusing the two will cost you too much. I had to make space. See it, taste it, feel it, and know this future intimately in your heart, and a new reality will then exist in your mind.

Purpose in the Pain

I always felt pulled by the future. In my talks, I often share how I felt dragged into a future that seemed preordained. I still feel this way. Nothing changed. There is a force demanding momentum that commands I build with the tools provided to me. This push to carve out the future where I could give back was hard to see at times. I kept moving forward, but I often did not have any clue where I was going.

Within months of my separation, years before we would finally be divorced, I resolved that I would lose everything. I was so busy trying to keep moving and succeed at this new multi-role of all things required to keep our lives going, that I was not connecting with the deep loss of hope for the future. I was not excited about where I was going. I was only surviving.

Less than two years later, I am reminded of having David on my team at the coaching company. David was working hard to make more money in a commission sales role. He would make a commission on event ticket sales, coaching, and product sales. And he would have times when he would be behind and had rent due.

He gave me a hard time when I first took over the company. His constant need to sabotage me was OK. I was willing to put up with that back then as I was not yet connecting his actions toward me as harming the greater good of the company. I remember the first time I tried to let him go. It ended up being a negotiation of empty promises and, later, regret.

Life carried on, and a few months later, we sat again face-to-face from each other. This time, there was no negotiation. David seemed insistent on hating everything we did, and I had bigger fish to fry turning around a broken company. He was costing us time, money, and energy that we could not afford to waste. David was let go that day. His attitude was bringing the whole team down, and I could not tolerate it.

Several months later, David reached out to my business partner, and my business partner recommended I take David back but left the final decision to me. I met with David to learn that he had started a new life. Divorced himself, he was seeing someone new, excited for a fresh start, and wanted to apologize. He had time to reflect on how hard I was trying to turn things around and regretted giving me such a hard time.

I hired David again, and within a few months, we were face-to-face once again. I was still a relatively new "manager" and had yet to see the writing on the wall. David was short on rent, again, and now had other mouths to feed and diapers to buy. I spoke with David about where he wanted to go. What did his future look like? What was he building toward? He replied that he was not like me. He did not have the resources to risk building something new, better, or different. He had responsibilities. For some reason, I carefully listened, empathized, and respected that we had different resources, conveniently forgetting where I was a less than twenty-four months before with my own mouths to feed, shelter to find, every cent frozen in joint accounts, and a new life to build. Maybe he was right. Maybe we were different. Maybe I was lucky or was denying my privilege as a white woman across from this equally white man. Did I have more access to money? Probably not. What about education? Mentorship? A supportive family? Or maybe I just wanted it more? All I knew is that I wanted to help David.

I offered to pay for a course, "Awaken Your Potential," focused on mindset and stepping into a leadership mentality. I offered him coaching and the opportunity to attend our training events. Months passed, and David would sit with me several times. I would give advances and even created a bonus a few times purposely to avoid adding to the "payback list." Many more times, I offered to cover courses and training. David believed that he simply could not afford to take the time to build a new vision of the future until he got his head above water with the reality he had. He was not working less than others. He had massive stress, and he needed the money and help as much as anyone. I would say he was in massive discomfort, and yet, he chose that same discomfort again every minute of every day that he kept his focus on the present. I may have stumbled into an unknown future many times. I made more mistakes than most. I had a lot of conditioning to undo from my upbringing, but, hey, who doesn't? The difference was that I kept reaching out, creating hope when I couldn't find any, and taking risks with the resources I had to create more.

I always believed my life was worth more than my personal self for as long as I can remember. There was always an adventure to be had, an experience to create, an odd to be beaten, and I happily stepped into the role of proving the peanut gallery wrong. If you are reading this book, I bet you beat the odds too. You overcome unbelievable challenges. You slayed dragons and sat in deep despair, and yet, here you are, in the eye of the storm, about to build, about to level up, with the only calm moment you have.

Maybe the difference between David and me was not resources, privilege, or bias at all; maybe it was simply what we believed. I believed the discomfort would mold me and take me somewhere better. I found purpose in pain.

You Can Bend Reality

Within six months of losing my house, my marriage, and available assets, I wrote a fresh letter to the future. This letter described the future only twelve months down the road, a life of love, happiness, resources, choices, and a successful rebuild for myself and my children. Only twelve months away, this new world waited for me. It was so close I could touch it in my mind and feel it in my heart. I would open that letter twelve months later from a completely new world. A world that I built in my mind before I calculated the dollars and cents, before I focused on the houses I would sell, or anything to do with my current circumstances. The letter was a clean slate, and every day that would pass from writing it would be in consistent alignment with the reality I was living in my mind.

I would write a letter from my future every year for the next decade. I still write one around New Year's Eve every year. The years of loss, like my separation; the six-month span where my life would be picked up by the world and thrown back down sideways when I lost my coaching company, my then partner in life, my best friend, along with most of my everyday acquaintances linked with my company; and again when I would discover I almost lost my new company to a leader misleading our team—in all of those times, I wrote the letter twice per year. I had to write it to cast an anchor to the future. I had to be the creator of my world. I knew what life looked like when it is left to others to decide your fate, and that is a risky business that is much too costly for me.

It is one of the most heart-filling and touching moments of my life every time I receive these letters from my clients. To be honoured and included in hearing their reactions when they open the letter a year later. To hear someone we helped exclaim the uncanny outcomes and to see the very wonder of this magical letter in creating their world. A year or two later, I will hear that the letter is sacred in their business/life planning regime, that they now realize they created the world that came to pass in their life. They now know my little secret, that I can and do bend reality in my favour. Simply seeing the results of imagining major aspects of your life into creation creates a secret magic in you. The confidence that comes from this magic is rock solid in its ability to take you into action and implementation. All of this done with a deep trust that with the best strategy, resources, and consistent action, you build the fate of your life. The energy and frequency of these wishes and dreams flow from our unconscious onto paper. With that pen in hand, we come as close as possible to the core of our purpose, our future, and the land where our desires, service, and contribution in this life are realized.

We are powerful. We are important. We build things that matter. When you can see a life of more time, money, and help you can rely on, when you can see, taste, and feel this new business that exists in your future, then you will act in alignment with the leader who already did it, with the exact blueprint, recipe, and values unique to your path. You will not be in balance, but you will carve the harmony of spending your time, money, focus, and resources on the things that matter to you most.

Go ahead and write your letter. Step into your future. It already exists, twelve short months, one year from now this life is waiting for you. Optimal, realistic, attainable, and important, this life will pull you through. Let this vision guide your everyday decisions, habits, goals, and who you give your ear to in your life. When you put pen to paper, get as detailed as possible. See yourself in this life one year from now. Get creative. Trust yourself. You already know where you are going and why.

The times when I was pulled into the future or David was pulled into the present, both not knowing where we were going— those times represent too great of a distance between the internal world of self, where we unconsciously create our world by default, and the external world of conscious minds, where we can design what we want.

The key is to align who you are and what you want with the perspective of your future self. If this idea of your future is too right-brain, creative, brain science, research-based, and proven for your left-brain to fathom, simply think of your current business hero, asking what would they think, say, believe, and do? How would they face the obstacles between today and twelve months from now?

This may seem out there and risky to you. I hesitated when I started to take the reins back and lead my own life. I resisted the letter from the future because it meant I was 100% responsible and that I could build the life I want. At the beginning, I was not sure I was ready to stop blaming life and others for my reality. I had a moment when I was so fed up with keeping things the same that I took a chance. I grabbed that moment and asked myself, "What better time could there be than now to carve out something better?"

I took the reins. Those moments defined my life, and they will define yours. It is just a letter, and if it is so far-fetched and out there, then what could it hurt to write one?

Chapter 5

THE MINDSET MATRIX
TO SUCCESS!

Myth: *I have a career in mortgage, real estate sales, and insurance.*

Truth: You operate a business, or you have a job. Most in sales do not realize they only have a job that stops paying when they stop working. The firm decision to operate a business is to decide to build something that pays you dividends.

R epeat after me: "My business has my back." Say it again— "My business has my Back!"

A business is very similar to a mind—it makes a better a servant than it does a leader. I am asking you to consider the power of taking the reins in your business to free up your time. You are in charge here. The investments you make in your business will allow you to expand or contract both your time and your money.

One of the biggest mistakes anyone in the sales industry can make is to assume that they are obsolete or have very little influence on the outcomes of their clients. Here are the assumptions salespeople use to make themselves obsolete every single day:

1. People will buy when they find the right house.
2. The client did not call me back, so I do not want to bug them.
3. People already know the importance of critical care and disability insurance.
4. The house will sell when it sells.
5. If they wanted a mortgage, they would have agreed to a credit check with me.
6. If they want to see homes, they will call.
7. People who are serious about buying investment properties are sure before they call.
8. We have better stock options and overall wealth advice; our clients should be more proactive if they want better results.
9. That buyer is totally illogical; they will never buy at that price. I am not wasting my time.

Anyone seasoned in the sales industry knows the vital role they play with a client one-on-one, and they believe

1. It is not a lead or a client's job to call.
2. People make decisions when they feel safe, secure, and confident.
3. We create trust and confidence with education.
4. How you explain things, and in what order, makes a massive difference in the outcome.
5. Cost is only an obstacle in the absence of value.
6. Never mix up the value you provide with the cost. Value comes first. Only then can the client understand cost.
7. People will choose the best of what is available if they trust the options in front of them.
8. You can know more, offer more, get superior results, and none of it will matter without the ability to effectively communicate with others.
9. We limit the market and our potential market share to our personal learning style, personality type, and perspectives until we know ourselves, and expand to understand and adapt to others.
10. Money is simply a value exchange. Provide more value, make more money.
11. The physical world does not lie. You are the best in your field but have no sales? You have the best team but no results? There is someone lying to themselves, but let's just say it is not the world lying to you.

It is so easy to see how we impact the outcomes with clients in our sales roles. We are vital to how many potential relationships turn into trusting clients and how long the client journey takes, whether our clients are prepared to act with confidence when the best opportunity presents itself or we proactively have the tough conversations to get things back on track as needed. In sales, we are coaches helping our clients solve problems and achieve their goals.

In your business, you need to take the reins in the same confident manner as you do in your sales role. You need to put your consultant's hat on and view your business from the air.

A few years ago, in *REM Magazine*, I described the different views of your business like this:

This is the moment. The game is down to the wire with both teams tied. You look left for a signal of the play that will take your team to the top, then to the right. You come to the frantic realization that you have no clue what play will save the day, no clue what the plays are, and no clue that you even needed them. Finally, you realize that a win will be fate or luck at best.

You ease your stance to assess the opposition. They must be in the same predicament, right? Wrong. They are standing tall and confident. They look to the sidelines and are signaled a play. Not only do they have a play, but they have a full book of the best strategies to win in the quickest amount of time. They have someone overseeing the game and signaling only after assessing the bigger picture. They have the playbook. You don't. It doesn't matter that you made the finals. You just lost the game and your top players for next season.

So, who are you in this example? You are probably a couple of different roles. If you are selling, you are the player on the field, also referred to as outside sales or operators. If you have a team, you are on the sidelines, hopefully with the playbook in hand, and referred to as Team Leader, CEO, Coach, or potentially Team Manager, Director of Sales, Director of Client Experience/Support, or Director of Operations Roles. You also own this business, which means you are looking for signals of a healthy business worth your risk, investment, delivering a healthy profit and/or return on investment (ROI).

The GCI Trap

I will never forget coaching with Jeff. This was several years ago, and Jeff was determined to have an online virtual office. At the time, he did not want to build a cohesive team, but more of a referral network where his online opportunities and spinoff business would be referred out to various agents for a referral percentage. Jeff and I went over how to compensate agents in our team model as well as the conversions we could achieve with agents if we trained, supported, and nurtured them versus just collecting a referral fee. Jeff had a clear goal, and that was to spend less time in the business and make the same money or more.

I knew Jeff was leaving a lot of money on the table for two reasons: he was simply collecting a referral fee for leads he created and nurtured, and he had very little influence on the actual results. There was very little tracking beyond a lead that was given, and we received a cheque whether the sale closed or not. When we started to review what Jeff was doing to organize the agents, create opportunities, and what he was making for his personal sales, I noticed two glitches in his numbers. Jeff was not paying himself anything for his role as team leader. Sure, Jeff was not fully fulfilling the role of team lead, which was in line with his desire to spend less time in the business, but he was also not being paid for what he was doing at all. Jeff was not calculating profit properly or at all.

Jeff was stuck in what I call the "GCI Trap" or the "Solopreneur Rut." He was taking everything he made on his personal sales and counting it as profit. The referrals from the other agents covered most of his expenses. In his mind, he was making good money at over $200k a year. Sure, he had some additional expenses over what the referral fees covered, but he was talking gross income paid to him personally.

Jeff was viewing the referrals as covering the cost of creating the marketing, the ad spends, and the cost of delivering leads to himself and his referral group of agents. But the reality is that Jeff could have made more money in less time working on his own. He was not calculating his time as team leader or the actual profit of the business. There was another serious problem with the return this business model was delivering to Jeff—he had very little influence on the results, as I mentioned before.

Jeff was distributing leads to agents with varying levels of success. He chose who to allow in his referral network, and all the agents had moderate to high levels of success in their field. Jeff assumed that agents at a decent level of production would convert the opportunities well. As time passed, we could see that this was not the case. The leads were not converted at the same rate that Jeff was able to convert a lead to a client, let alone to a paid deal. This meant that the cost of a client and cost of a deal was much higher for Jeff the minute he sent a lead to one of the referral agents. These leads were also leaving his database, so he had no way of knowing if they were being contacted later by the agent at all. We did not even get into quality control, values, or ensuring these valuable opportunities were being served at a level Jeff was comfortable with or that represented his passion for client experience and superior service.

I still remember the call when Jeff said, "Wait a minute, are you saying I should be paid separately for being a Team Leader? You mean more than what I make for my sales?"

Not only did we need to allocate income for key Team Leader tasks once the business was big enough to warrant them, but we also needed to stop looking at what Jeff made as gross income just for him. This perception was holding him back, and it holds back millions of people in sales industries across North America.

Part of the difficulty is looking to expand your business from the perspective of someone selling in it. This perspective will keep you stuck. The views from on the field, from the coach's bench, from the stands, and the owner's box are very different. You do not need to be all the people in your business or fill all the roles. However, you *do* want to create a strategy for growth using one specific perspective. Hint: It is not the view from the field.

When you walk into a retail store, no one assumes the person who helps you pick out that new pair of shoes pockets the full ticket price. This seems silly and naive in a retail environment. Yet, in sales, we *are* awarded for gross sales income, also known as the full ticket price, of the service we provide. We claim our income as a full paycheck when a deal is done. This makes no sense. You pay fees to be in your business, you have marketing, potentially administration, database, software, client retention, client experience, training, coaching, and various other expenses before you get your cut.

The self-employed solopreneurs tell themselves they are making $200k when the stunningly successful business owners will assess the same business speaking a totally different language. This new language matters. Business owners have a different perspective of a healthy business and the ability for that business to grow. They organize the business and the money differently. They speak the language of net income for their role in the business and profit for ownership. Business owners will look at the same books and see $100k net earnings to you, $200k gross earnings, and no profit.

Perspective on Earnings	Solopreneur Mindset	Business Owner Mindset
Gross Earnings	$200,000	$200,000
Expenses (Example: Salaries, Marketing, Broker Fees, Client Retention, Reserves, Operational Costs, Debt, Credit)	Perceived as $0	-$100,000

Income Before Taxes	Perceived as $200,000	$100,000
Taxes (Corporate and/or Personal Tax Example)	-$20,000	-$20,000
Profit or Net Business Income	Perceived as $200k actually $80K	$80,000

Let me explain. You are the business and have no one else bringing in funds, so this takes profit off the table. You make $200k, you pay $100k in overall expenses, and you paid yourself the full $100k leftover in net income before taxes which means nothing was left in the company to create a profit as taxes are being deducted from your full income.

If you are an incorporated business, you may leave funds in the incorporation as profit, but the reality is that right now you are likely saving that "profit" for your retirement by utilizing the tax shelter that a corporation may afford you. You most likely still see this money as income being placed in a sheltered savings account. This is very different from owning a business that pays all key players at market value for their work, including your role, with net income after all those people and expenses are paid. Profit is after taxes once all those key players and expenses are paid, regardless of whether you work in this business or not.

This way of organizing your budgets, profit and loss, and overall thoughts about the financial side of the business is your key to expansion because it makes the views from the field, the sidelines, and the owner's box visible all at once. You cannot build what you cannot see. This is how implementors work with leverage to do less personally, make more money, and create teams they can count on.

Today, Jeff runs one of the largest teams in the country for a major brand with sales support to ensure he has as much time to work in the business, on the business, and to live his life away from the business. The biggest take away he got from our coaching was the transition from solo to entrepreneur and business owner. Planting these seeds today are the key to your time freedom and expansion tomorrow.

I had to work through similar things Jeff experienced when I started to work with Mikayla. She wanted to be more efficient. Mikayla was a top producer in her industry for two decades, but she felt like her business was too disorganized to identify the high-priority tasks. There was no team yet and no other salespeople yet, but she had a massive need for leverage and to get some time back so she could expand her business.

Now, we knew what her time with clients, face-to-face, was worth to the business. We also knew what it would cost to move clients to other salespeople if Mikayla ever wanted to sell less or stop selling altogether. We built this model on business principles that every small business needs to adhere to in order to stay afloat and keep their accounts in the black.

We used the KBCC Economic Model & Compensation Creation Strategy to first evaluate all the roles Mikayla was hiring herself to cover in her business. We needed to know what she was doing, what she loved, and what Mikayla was still hanging onto and doing herself that could be moved to someone else.

We explored the mistake most solo salespeople make in thinking they are earning the gross amounts on their paychecks before expenses and deductions. This allowed Mikayla to see a few things. One, she was making much less than she thought in take-home income, and we flipped this to get help and make more. Two, she was not making critical reinvestments in the right places based on her income level, and this was costing her expansion opportunities. Third, she could assess how well she was performing with the leads and opportunities the business was creating. Would she hire herself with the present rate of return, or would she be comfortable hiring someone else performing at her same level or less?

That may get confusing depending on how often you are exposed to the business owner mindset. Therefore, some business owners become stunningly successful when they enter the Mindset Matrix of a successful business owner. All of a sudden, everything looks different. What was once a task you loathed can now be done better and for a fraction of the cost. What was your Achilles heel becomes an opportunity to leverage and improve. We can create a system for everything with the right help and have happier clients. Until you have a foundation of capable people who can finesse and improve what you have built, look for the people who can get it done and implement a proven playbook for how to get it done

Essentially, with Mikayla, we did a few matrix mindset flips to see the business differently. We looked at net income. Then we looked at what she would make if she was a sales agent paid with the structure we created for her team. We looked at what would be done with the remaining portion of the sale earnings that went to the team. We reviewed where we would invest so the sales agents had fewer tasks to do overall, but the tasks they did were in alignment with their typical personalities and strengths. The tasks they did not typically do well went to team support roles. This meant the sales agents would have more time and more opportunities to fill that time with face-to-face client opportunities.

Next, I asked a few important questions that typically cause a head tilt for most leaders. You will do all of this to support the sales agents on your team: you will take away what they will typically dislike doing, allowing them to do more of what they like doing and increasing the opportunities for them to make more money. If you agree that the business will subsequently have a higher net income, why not do it now for yourself? Why not free up your time for more face-to-face opportunities for yourself? Why not give yourself a raise in time and money as well?

Typically, this is met with fear and questions like, "But my sales income will cover everything just in case," and, "Don't we need multiple agents first?" or, "I can't afford to hire help until our sales are up."

All of these are fair questions to ask in the GCI solopreneur world. In the world of leverage and team, you have a mental edge in calculating your personal sales income just as anyone else would be paid on your team and investing the rest as you would when expanding the business with other sales agents. This investment will produce growth, but one of the biggest reasons this hack works is mental. You will be hiring help and have more time as you are now making less per deal in pay per hour, taking more time with the help you now have. The reality of your net income might have caused some unease, and the reality of now paying yourself as all team members will be paid per deal will likely create a bit of scarcity where you feel you need to sell more to earn what you need to live. This is the perfect combination. Often, we hire help and take 100% of the extra time for our personal life. After the pinch months of hiring, training, and selling, most are relieved for a break. This is totally understandable. But what we really want is to decide how much of our time needs to be replaced with new client opportunities. You will instantly have a raise, as those face-to-face client activities are worth more to the business. What felt like a risk just made you money.

That year, Mikayla had her best year in sales ever, and the next year, she exceeded those numbers for a new best. She already had administrative and some marketing support in place. By the end of year one, the clarity of her roles and perspective in the business allowed her to bring on help with sales as well to free up valuable time on the weekends and in the evening while she spent time with her children.

Those who are stunningly successful live in a different universe of business, and I want you to see the world through the lens of possibility versus frustration, obstacles, and blocks.

Cheating yourself out of your best life, trading a top-1-% life for the much lower destination of only a top 1% business is missing the mark altogether. You have one life to explore, discover, create, and hopefully leave a legacy in service. I relish in my alone time, and even I know being on a yacht solo is only happy for so long.

Being in the top 1% of producers only matters when you have a top 1% life to go with it, and that means having someone else on your boat with you.

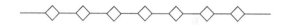

Chapter 6

ADDICTED TO LEVERAGE:
THE GENIUS METHOD

I first met Sarah at a leadership event, and she was ready to quit her business. Quality of life was not a term matching the present depiction of her life. To say she was fed up would be an understatement. All signs pointed to burnout being on the horizon, and the panic was evident.

Sarah and her husband Ben worked so hard to build a strong business. They now had a young son and wanted some time at home, so they took steps to leverage some administrative tasks and found someone to help. This took months of training and time from Sarah, but she finally had a taste of the freedom and confidence that a support position provides. She could do more than before and get things done faster for clients and herself.

Quickly, Sarah and Ben got busier. They used this newly-found free time in a few different ways. They reinvested by launching new lead generation and client experiences. They also refined current marketing to increase the volume of leads coming into the business, and they spent more time at home with their son.

The newfound freedom was making them slightly more in net income than before. It seemed amazing to take on a salary only to earn more, both gross and net. Sure, it took months of attempted training, and there was no time to create the operations manuals they imagined, but they were in business! They had leverage, and it felt good.

However, when the help they thought they could rely on left, Sarah and Ben were given little to no notice to allow for a game plan. Even a week would have allowed them to assign more of the administrator's time to creating some written instructions or even a daily to-do list. All those training hours spent and they were left feeling further behind than when they started. There was next to nothing documented to recreate the position for the next hire. For several months, Sarah and Ben decided to get by without help, and the end result was they felt run off their feet.

Have you ever had someone you rely on leave suddenly? I am placing my odds on a "yes" here. Who wasn't left high and dry a few times in their lives? Well, for an entrepreneur, a.k.a. small- to medium-sized business owner, this is your worst nightmare. It's scary to be fully booked and, all of a sudden, have to spend time on financially valuable tasks that someone else was doing. This fear can be so strong that it once again feels safer, easier, and less time-consuming to just do things yourself.

By the time I met Sarah at the real estate event, she was so desperate, she was willing to try anything. It turned out that trying anything included the system which is now known as the KBCC Ultimate Expansion Strategy that would help them gain clarity in their leverage.

Mission Accomplished

Leverage goes wrong when you lack clarity. When you hand things over to people who do not care or know what your wish for success is, lack the care or training on your proven systems, and lack the personal experience to create the results you want to see, everything fails. It might not fail on day one, but trust me, it will fail.

You either hire for Genius, share what you have, and get the heck out of the way, or you hire for talent, values, and train for skill. Hiring for talent and training for skill makes sense for rudimentary tasks, checklists, and systems that you need done a certain way to empower the whole business. Leadership roles requiring Genius—meaning talent, skill, passion, and purpose—come later; those positions are a higher investment for work that is more valuable to the business, and more difficult to replace.

These roles will be your key to scaling with a leadership team you trust and enjoy working with, and they will be key to your next levels of expansion.

Leverage is the ultimate leadership tool, and it is also the ultimate team system. A great team looks for personality types, talents, and skills that will empower a team member to meet or exceed expectations for their role. Everyone wins when Sarah and Ben hire Candice, who kills it at social media, loves doing it, and does a better job than Sarah and Ben even when they had time! With a team, there is no competition; there is only winning at your role toward a greater good.

Sarah and Ben went from an over $200k business to seven figures with a team of seven in less than five years. The mark of success was not the seven figures, though. The mark of success was a seven-day vacation with zero business activity and zero need for their phones. Mission accomplished!

Building with Confidence

But how do you get over the fear that is so strong, it stopped Sarah from hiring again? How do you get over that fear of having someone leave when you're unprepared, the fear of having your time wasted training someone, and that fear of being used and unappreciated? Or that ultimate fear of looking unprepared and even incompetent to clients and colleagues?

Loss of control can be one of the hardest aspects of building a business for some people, particularly for certain leadership and personality styles. For strong drivers, their biggest fear is losing control.

Here is one of the exercises Ben and Sarah did as we sought clarity on whether they should hire again and how to hire the right person with a strong plan to quickly bring someone else on after if needed. I want you to get a pen and paper out and write a list of all the things you need to do for your business and life on a daily, weekly, and monthly basis. Then, I want you to rate your ability to do the tasks on your list. You may need to add to this list over a week to consciously recall all the things you do.

I am asking you to list personal and business on purpose. This is an exercise to find clarity in the world of leverage. Some of the heaviest and most costly tasks my clients held onto, which limited their time, energy, and money, were on the personal side. We know women still do a disproportionate share of the household duties, and even when they have help with those duties, they still oversee the weight of managing and delegating those tasks. The house is essentially another business altogether, and you need to run that business also. If this is not a factor for you, then that will be obvious when you score your list.

I have thousands of agents where the home and business tasks required of them exceeded the hours in their days, and they could not figure out why they were so tired and felt like they were working all the time. If unloading the dishwasher and doing laundry is a five out of ten on your hourly energy scale and connecting face-to-face with clients or spending time with your family is a two out of ten and maybe even renews your energy, then you only have two options:

1. Change how you think about laundry and the dishwasher, or

2. Stop demoting yourself in time and energy!

Is your prosperity higher with your family or face-to-face with clients? How much would it cost for someone to do laundry, dishes, and some light (or extensive) cleaning per week? I will let you do the comparison on this.

Because you picked up this book, I am assuming you have a decent, and probably quite successful, business. I am figuring you are dropping extra opportunities or could easily buy or make more opportunities; otherwise, with time or money, you could increase the opportunities that make you money. Is that right? Great! That means you have gold sitting on the curb as garbage waiting for pick up and are spending your time counting pennies. Remember the gumballs? You have enough to buy them now, so stop counting change and go for the gold!

The KBCC GENIUS Method

Step 1 of the exercise is writing a list of all the tasks you are doing daily, weekly, and monthly, both in business and necessary tasks in your personal life also.

Step 2 includes rating your ability to do the tasks on your list using the KBCC GENIUS Method, which I will describe to you below.

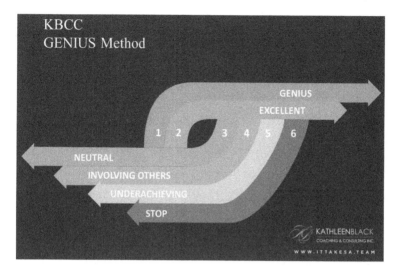

G: Genius

These tasks make the business the most money because they provide you or your clientele the most value. These tasks should energize, excite, and propel you. You are passionate about these tasks and it shows. Your energy is contagious. You can complete these tasks with greater ease than most people. You may identify these tasks in an area where you are talented. You want to do these tasks. You are extraordinary at them and consistently get results. You will practice and invest to master these tasks. You will see subtle nuances that others do not understand because of your depth of talent, skill, or knowledge in these areas.

E: Excellent

You enjoy these tasks and are good at them. You get above average results with these tasks and could easily fill a day doing them. You worked to become better at these tasks and may improve on them if needed, but they do not bring the same joy and passion as your Genius tasks.

N: Neutral

You will do these tasks when necessary. They are fillers for you, not high priority projects. You do not feel you do these tasks better than average, or better than others, but they need to get done and you do them.

I: Involving Others

You intended to have someone else do these tasks for you, but never let go of the reigns. You do not trust the other person to complete the task to your standards without you, or the person insists on your involvement. Make no mistake: this is not collaboration; this is not productive; this is failed delegation. These tasks are where you are letting the business pull you back in and away from your Genius.

U: Underachieving

These are tasks that you know you are not fantastic or even average at. They may also be tasks that you are not even aware that you're incompetent at. Otherwise, these tasks are your own personal enemy holding you back, and you have not yet identified them to do anything about it. They are out of your awareness and holding you back. You can't know what you don't know. The key is to see the time and energy drain a task takes for you. Also, consistent training, coaching, and accountability will help you to see these areas of weakness and help you turn them into strengths by leveraging the Genius of others.

S: Stop

You know these tasks are a train wreck in your business. No need to mince words here. Doing these items outright drains you. You avoid these tasks, they build up, and they create urgent issues that you must fix later. Stop doing this to yourself and your business. Doing these tasks are costing you money and will cost you growth. If you really feel like flexing the work-harder muscle, you can train to improve and force yourself to perform, but how is that leveraging to make you more money or getting you more time? Just Stop.

Step 3: Write down the average number of hours you spend doing each task weekly. Now, if this is strictly a once-a-month task, you just need to divide the hours by four. Keep this super simple and make all time calculations per week. If you must drive to complete the task, include travel time. If you have to plan prior to the task, include time for that.

Step 4: Add up all the hours you rated as N, I, U, or S. How many hours a week are you spending doing things that you are below excellent at?

Step 5: Now calculate how many of the hours in Step 4 require some type of licensing in your profession. You do not want to go into how a licensed or certified person would be better trained to complete the task better. This is simply about whether a person would have to be legally licensed or certified, based on the rules and regulations of your profession, to perform this specific task.

Compare the hours on your list from Step 4 that require a license/certification versus those that do not. You most likely have a longer list which does not require the certification or license. In that case, you will want to find leverage with someone to help who does not have a license/certification in your field.

However, for some of you, the list will be even or tipped in the other direction. You have an interesting choice. What is more important to you? To create a business that can support other stand-alone sales roles, other people to sell like you now and later; or to build a business that allows you to do more in the short-term but still relies on you 100% in the long-term?

For example, in real estate, a strong listing agent can double business with a licensed assistant. Once they double their business, they will have far less time to create the systems, recruit, train, and expand other salespeople compared to the agent who hires an unlicensed administrator for far less in cost to the company and creates a smooth process for all unlicensed tasks in the meantime. That smooth process for unlicensed tasks creates a value-rich offer for other sales agents to join your business now and later. There is value to others in working with the support platform you will have built for unlicensed tasks.

It all depends on what you want now versus what you want later. Again, do you want to create a business that can support other stand-alone sales roles and have the option to sell less yourself one day, or do you want to build a business that allows you to do more in the short-term but still relies on you 100% in the long-term?

Step 6: Put a price on it. What are all those tasks from the list you created in Step 4 worth on an hourly basis? Is this a full-time or part-time salary? Divide it to come up with an hourly cost. Is this a service? Divide all fees per week or month to come up with an hourly cost for the service to do these tasks for you. We will call this weekly amount "*Cost.*"

If you had some tasks requiring a license/certification but more that did not require it, deduct the hours requiring certification from your list. If you had more requiring a license, you can keep the whole list and count all the hours for now.

When calculating market value, keep in mind that rates may be less hiring someone in house versus leveraging out, but also some tasks may not require full-time hours or require greater levels of Genius, meaning an outsourcing service would save you money with a better overall result.

Step 7: Now for the hard part. How many hours are you working in your business? Calculate a realistic number of hours worked per week and multiply that by the number of weeks you work per year. So, if you take four weeks off for vacation or holidays, etc. you would take your weekly number of hours multiplied by forty-eight. Those total working hours will be called "*Time.*"

You are not tricking anyone but yourself if you try to say you work more or less hours. Be accurate about how much you are actually working. Remember, this is an exercise in leverage. I don't care how many hours you work or how many you want to work; I care that you have a viable plan to get you where you want to go.

Step 8: Now I want you to do three things:

1. Take your gross earnings in the last twelve months or the prior calendar year. You want the total earnings, before expenses, taxes or deductions for the most recent twelve-month range that you have access to. We will call this *Gross.*
2. *Gross* divided by *Time* = Your Gross Personal Hourly Wage
3. Now take your *Net* earnings in the most recent twelve-month span you have access to for accurate numbers. This may be your tax return; if so, go down to the earnings after deductions but before taxes. You want the total earnings after expenses and deductions but before taxes for the most recent twelve-month range that you have access to. We will call this *Net.*

Net divided by *Time* = Your Personal Net Hourly Wage (before taxes)

Because of incorporation versus self-employed options, I will not be getting into net after taxes, but I recommend you calculate that for yourself. Bringing on help for tasks in your business is an expense or deduction which will reduce your net earnings. This could also reduce your taxes paid overall, but that is not our focus here. Our focus is to make more and have more time overall, which will increase gross and net earnings from where they are now.

Net after taxes divided by *Time* = Your Personal Net hourly Wage

Step 9: Now for the moment of truth. Let's compare.

Take Your gross hourly wage deducted by the hourly *Cost* you created in Step 6.

A. *Gross*: Your Gross Personal Hourly Wage is _____
B. *Cost*: Gross Hourly Cost of Help is _____

Are you making more money per hour in your personal gross hourly income than the *Cost* to bring in reliable help per hour? If so, congratulations! As long as you can create more paid sales opportunities in the time you used to spend doing the N, I, U, S tasks, you can give yourself a raise!

If you are making less money per hour in your personal gross hourly income than the *Cost* to bring in reliable help per hour, you need to increase your personal sales volume with better conversion, overall sales volume, or decrease current expenses. Explore the data in your business to pinpoint exactly where you can make changes to get to a place where your gross personal hourly is higher than help. This is vital to lean into educated risk, which will give you more time and money. How do I know this? The numbers are already skewed in your favour. If you take your overall hours worked from Step 7 and deduct your hours spent in N, I, U, and S tasks from Step 4, then divide your gross earnings by this reduced number of hours, which is your actual hourly rate on the GENIUS plan, your GENIUS tasks are worth much more to the business on an hourly basis. We are not even touching excellent level activities yet. As you start to leverage tasks off your plate, you will discover there is repeatedly a new reorganization of what is now at each G-E-N-I-US category. Perspective is everything, and the perspective changes when you have clarity on what your time is worth in money and quality of life.

Let's take Sarah and Ben. Assuming their gross income was $250,000 minimum in gross earnings and they both worked 60 hours a week, their hourly wage was $43.40 each. Now, they hire Sarah, who is making $20 an hour for 30 hours a week. This is a modified example, as we have two agents, but essentially Sarah and Ben now make $33.40 for the hours they are not working and are using the time to bring more clients into the business. Soon, they are back up to their full rate and exceeding it as their work time as sales agents generates a higher income overall and per hour. If you are spending 50% of your working hours doing unlicensed tasks, you could potentially double your business, or you could choose to increase the business by 30% with 30% more clientele and 30% more gross profit. Your worth goes up again per hour, and you now have 20% of the time that was spent in your business for your personal life and a raise.

Do you see how this works? We did not even attempt to adjust for the increased efficiency of having someone who has, potentially, more talent, interest, and excitement for the unlicensed tasks than you do. With the right person in the role, that person will do more at a higher quality level, leaving time for new projects which also help you build a better client experience, more referrals, and that person also ends up helping to build the business with you! You will have more energy, time, and money. Leverage gives you the ability to be two or three people at once, only better. Everyone wins!

One day, you may imagine multiple people covering the various aspects of your business. You will start to see your business as a team helping people, and that help will equate to goodwill and value being deposited into the market. That value is the energy of money.

When a team helps more people, creates more value, and makes more money, it moves from being a business all about supporting you to a business about supporting your team, which then supports your clients. When that happens, your personal hourly wage will become irrelevant as you will step into the Mindset Matrix. You will go from hourly worker trading time for money to a team trading value for income. The quicker you can see the business as its own whole entity with expenses and earnings for all roles—even yours—and a resulting value earned per year, the quicker you will be on your way to becoming addicted to leverage.

So, let's say you have leverage. How do you leverage better?

Find Your Edge

You were built to win, which means you were made precisely to live your journey and build something the world needs. The refinement of your personal self into your best self is part of the path that every leader will walk.

To find your edge, you need to know yourself. You need to know yourself so well that you can make quick decisions on where to put your time, money, focus, and energy to live in excellent and Genius-level activities as much as possible. You need to know yourself so well that you leverage or delegate without guilt, restraint, or self-judgement. No one is good at everything! Knowing this changes the view from doing everything better to doing what you do best better and empowering others at everything else.

You need to know yourself so well that you can stand in who you are without feeding the dragons. Remember, the world will feed off your uncertainty. When you are uncertain, own it; take the time you need and find the resources to move you forward without hesitation. You do not owe anyone an explanation.

You need to know who you are to recognize that a lot of the world is not like you. Others will not lead like you, communicate like you, and often will not reason like you. These realities can be very painful. When I shared that I had to stop feeding the dragons with dripping, raw pieces of my heart and that I needed to stop asking others who were not me to say being me was OK, there was another very important reason I had to stop feeding the dragons: their scorn.

If you are reading this book, you are strong, you are building; you are in the world of doing, learning, and leaning into risk and challenge. Women like that can rub people the wrong way. The scorn of, "Who the heck did I think I was to venture into turning a business around, selling real estate, or building a new business as a single woman and single mom? Who the heck was I to have the audacity to take on the world?"

That was the key. Eventually, I knew who I was, and I knew it rubbed in the face of everyone who was not doing what their journey called them to do. I believed in myself enough, and that really pissed people off. If they were not criticizing me, they were saying it was all impossible; and, worse yet, throwing extra challenges to try to break me. I guess if they broke me, it would feel better to be broken themselves. Broken and still. I will take broken in motion any day. But broken and still? You are basically dead, my friend. I have the audacity to revere life more than that. I was built to win and was telling myself that my whole life. Trust me, no one else was telling me that I was built to win; so, I did, and now I am telling you. You are 100%, without a doubt, unequivocally born to win, so keep going!

Understand Others

The way to understand others will sound somewhat backward, but the journey is back to knowing yourself. I bet, as a child, you never knew that others processed their emotions, beliefs, and perception of the world differently than you did. The reality is that we have different ways to learn, process energy, deal with stress, and emotionally respond in the only world we know: the one in your head.

There is no other world. You will never fully know this world from the eyes of another human being. We try. You are reading a book right now written through my eyes. This could be good or bad for you. For those of you looking to leverage and grow, this is good for you, because I am an odd duck built precisely for the world of mindset, optimization, systems, leverage, expansion, defying the odds, overcoming risk, and growing through the pain. I was built for this, and that is why I can help you.

For some of us, learning to know yourself is freedom and pain. Like most people, I always felt different. To feel different is normal. Imagine that! In fact, most people feel different, particularly in the entrepreneurial pool. Even with this normal mentality of feeling different, my life was often in chaos as I failed to calculate why people would do what they would do. Years later, I would discover a personality type focused on task completion and precision. It was no surprise to discover that this personality mix had a relatively low representation by the global population.

I once met an individual at an Neural Linguistic Programming (NLP) training and happened to sit across from him at lunch when it slipped out of his mouth that his DISC personality type is DC, same as mine. "DC's run the world," he said. I am sure he was half-joking, but in truth, we cannot help but see all of the moving pieces with a love to seamlessly connect them for unlimited growth. Our minds see all things as forever connected; we want it done yesterday and can drive a project forward despite hurdles, but we want it done to the ultimate of results. This level of idealism gets it done, albeit with a few victims lying wounded in the process.

Myers Briggs allowed me to see that I am 0.08% of the female population and less than 2% of the overall population.

This frustration of my life was starting to make sense, as was the justification of others for my results. Well, of course, she is unique and different; that is why she built the companies she has for clients and for herself. Unfortunately, people love to find excuses they can claim to be legitimate for their own lack of results. Think about it. You must have a secret advantage; and if you do, it makes sense that I could never achieve what you did. It couldn't be hard work. It must be an unfair advantage the rest of us cannot access. In the team world, this does not exist. Accessing your own gifts is just the beginning. The only cap is from a failed ability to access the mindset and leverage you needed.

Every personality must work what they have until they have the resources to leverage what they need. Most people just wait too long to start. To be different is a lonely path at times, but also satisfying. I want you to know who you are to lead yourself with confidence first and to then lead others to an outcome together. They will not do it like you, because if you leverage right, they will not be like you. We already have you! Think strong well-rounded foundation who all agree on the cathedral they are building versus the shack they could throw up together.

You want to know others and yourself well enough to stay in your lane moving forward. All this time spent going back and forth, second-guessing, and beating yourself up mentally could all be funneled directly forward; and for that, you need clarity.

You were built for unique gifts I may be lacking, but I am only lacking if I do not have someone else to balance it all out for me. Solo, your lack runs the risk of shinning brighter than your talents.

In a team, your talents are your contribution, allowing your Genius to shine exponentially brighter.

There is an amazing number of assessments and inventories you can take to know yourself: DISC, KOLBE, Myers Briggs, NLP Representational Systems, Values Levels, Emotional Intelligence (EQ), and so many more. Every time you expand your perspective of how you think, what makes you move and tick, you are also moving forward to know others. The more you see who you are in comparison to the world, the more you understand how varied the world is.

I rely heavily on a few key assessments in supporting you while you prepare to get reliable help, trying to motivate and manage. I also rely on gathering lessons from when someone may leave your business and you want to adapt and communicate better with similar employee profiles in the future. Being doomed to repeat the past is the opposite of systematic thinking. You want to be empowered to never live that error again and make the whole system better because it happened.

The top assessments I recommend for team building are DISC personality profiles. DISC allows us to divide focus between tasks, relationships, and expressive and less expressive personality types. With these four areas of focus, we can understand the way we naturally see the world and the way we are adapting to fit our environments. We can assess pace, results, and whether our clients, our teams, or ourselves value who, what, how, or why the most in decision making. Every DISC personality type has a prime directive. We assess the ideal profile for every role prior to hiring and adjust coaching/training to the team leader and the team members' personalities for far greater success. I used these extensively for well over a decade and can often pinpoint a profile as soon as we start coaching together. We adapt our coaching and training by personality and know who will be climbing a steep cliff with as they attempt to step into the mentality of someone successful in the role they are training to fill. Many roles in the business, when done well, are built from specific personality perspectives. This is a secret weapon when hiring. You match the role to the perfect mindset to achieve the tasks and identify the ideal personality profile. From there, you know who can flex and how far before the transition in perspectives is just too painful for them.

Every personality style and learning style brings valuable input. The drivers are louder and more vocal, but that does not make them the best perspective for operations, efficiency, tracking, or assessing the longevity of a new program. Often, the first to speak up are visual learning styles and dominant drivers, and while their opinions and insight are vital, they are likely to miss essential aspects to scaling a business that feel whole with a solid foundation you can grow upon. I have a variety of experts in various areas of business growth on my team. They all have personalities matching their unique expertise. This is fantastic for a successful outcome. However, when you have a leader who does not know how or herself, that leader will try to be all things to all people and push away the very expertise that is often needed.

You cannot leverage strength you cannot see and understand. A team needs all personality perspectives to build a strong whole.

We are not talking about mindset, beliefs, or abundance mentality here; we are talking about the way one processes the world and finds fulfillment. Let someone who loves structure, process, and efficiency help you build the systems you need to run your business.

Lots of leaders leverage out training, systems creations, and strategic insights. It is also common for many leaders to be drivers. Eventually, they learn that they are often the biggest hurdle to building for a variety of reasons. You need to know these reasons as a driver to protect yourself before you wreck yourself. As an operator or salesperson, you need to know these reasons to work effectively with drivers and bring in the drivers you need by hiring and coaching.

Live the GENIUS Method

Do what you love, do your Genius tasks, and I bet you will make more money. That bet comes from over seventeen thousand hours of personal coaching time plus the time of multiple coaches on my coaching teams. This is not a fair bet. I have insider knowledge. What you love creates more value to the world. If you love administrative work, find agents who want to work for your ultimate support system and become part of your team. Over time, you can train them yourself or buy proven training and slowly sell less of yourself. For most of you reading this, it will be the opposite, and you will sell more or work on building the overall business more, but the equation still works.

Leverage is the ultimate human and business expansion tool. To see a task, vision, dream, or movement come to fruition is one of the most beautiful experiences I ever witnessed. You can build a business from negative six figures, from nothing, or with outside investment, or with partners investing together. In the end, it doesn't matter where you start. It matters if you have a strong strategy and if you have the guts to do the least-risky, most-resisted, fear-inducing aspect of getting your time back: leveraging GENIUS!

It is riskier not to leverage. I hope this chapter built your confidence and flipped the script on leveraging help. What takes ten years to create and perfect takes only two years to replicate and implement with the expertise that created it. Do the math on that in your business. Your competition is not getting ahead on its own. They are on the golf course because they have help doing the very things keeping you in the office.

Chapter 7

YOUR VALUES, YOUR STANDARDS, YOUR REPUTATION, DONE YOUR WAY

Leverage

"The use of tools and resources to do more with less effort, saving time and money without sacrificing your standards of service."

I n the definition for leverage included above that my company has used for eleven years, you might notice that it does not say to do more at the expense of your standards of service. To further clarify, this definition says, "Without sacrificing your standards of service." The reality is that you have a unique way of operating in your business. Some of the ways that you do things are unique to you. Things like your personality, sense of humour, volume of business, and communication style are all part of the way you personally express yourself in business. Others do not need to be trained in these aspects of you when you hire. Whoever you hire will have an art of their own.

Other aspects of your business allowed you to build a strong reputation, which is invaluable to the business. These pieces are the science of your business and include your values, marketing, frequency of communication with clients, services, beliefs, work ethic, knowledge base, wording for calls and emails, and unique approach to the way you support a client. These aspects, which we want to train any new hire on, are the science of your business. Tapping into the science of your business is the key to getting the kind of help that you can rely on.

At McDonalds, Starbucks, and The Keg, the science is in the recipes, order of service, pace, menus, branding, dress code, marketing, dispute resolution standards, hiring processes, employee pay scales, pricing, and the carefully crafted duplicatable experience; and if it all works, there is a consistent high quality experience for the client as planned by the brand. Whereas the accent of a server, their smile, the warm way about them, and the joke they may tell at the table are all a personal art. The rude server, the disgruntled manager, the distracted retail associate, and the one-off advertising flyer that looked like it was a Bi-Way knock off—those are all art, too, but done to the detriment of the brand science. Art and science are important. The science protects the whole, and the art is designed to complement the whole. If one person's unique take on pay, marketing, or company values compromises the strength of the whole for the rest of the team, you have a problem. You may hire while acknowledging the advantages of art and talent, but they do not make for a successful franchise; they add to it or take away from it, but they do not make it successful. On the flip side, if the art of one person is what makes your business successful, you are in for some trouble, The science has to be strong—that is the systematic and strategic core of the business; that is your vision and implementation of where you are going.

Leadership by Fire

If everyone set out to build a thriving, profitable, efficient team with the goal of selling it one day, business building would be a lot easier. We would be all in to build exactly what would allow us to exit and sell. It would mean systems, processes, and culture are your only solutions. You would not have the option to carry the business because it would cost you the entire endgame. It would cost you the very goal that led you to be in the business in the first place.

On the odd occasion, I worked with clients in this position. They knew their strengths and often had a partner with a different personality type, allowing them the freedom to build while their partner held sales. They were not 100% sure if they wanted to stop selling or if they wanted to sell the business one day. What they did know made their situation perfect for growth, though. They knew they wanted choices.

If you don't if know you want to sell the business, or stop selling, or have someone else lead the team, that is totally OK. But you need to be committed to building a business that delivers you the option to do any of those things. That is the key to building together with greater ease.

You need to be clear about what you want to have to give you the edge to do what you need to do. The world will not hand you the business you want; it will hand you the business it thought you needed when you called out on a whim that day, and then change its mind again tomorrow when you do. No one wins building a business floating in like a feather. I live for flow, energy, inspired direction, and I also know that you will not move forward without telling the world your deepest wishes. You will not move forward without carving the walls of the river that hold your energy for your energy and flow to move with ease in the direction you desire. You set the pace or current, but the world helps you carve the way. Tell the world and yourself clearly and specifically what you want.

The reality is that most people do not get help in their business because they have this beautiful vision of a salable business. Most people get help to breathe again. They feel like they are underwater, cringing at the thought of any additional commitments over what is already on their plate. Often, they tried to hire help in some capacity and ended up working more hours, only for the hire to eventually leave with little notice. Now, they are swimming in what we categorized as a "S: Stop" task in the GENIUS Model. This is a task they should not be doing anymore, and they need help now more than ever, but they don't want to need help. They are in the fire and don't want the fire department. But the house is on fire. They have to do something!

That is where I meet a lot of people. The fire is doing damage to the business, their energy, their enthusiasm, their health, and their family. They feel like they are letting everyone down, and others are trying to help, often with misguided but well-intentioned advice. Someone might have sent the "perfect" hire your way, and in desperation, you are considering it and reaching out, longing to find some sense of control in the process.

This is leadership by fire. What do you do in a burning house? Run, find shelter, and look for help to extinguish the flames. You are not thinking about rebuilding when your eyes are ablaze with flames. The trouble with business building is that you are often still trying to salvage a model long burnt to the ground over investing in the plans, finalizing the finishes, and getting on with building a better model that actually works.

When One Is Not Enough

A few years ago, I had something interesting happen. There was a trip that took the top 1% producers from across the country on a world-class vacation together. They spent several days sightseeing, masterminding, and getting to know each other. There were a few teams that had built the foundations of their business with me who took part on the trip. As the teams began to compare notes, some interesting facts came out for both the teams who built with me and the teams who had not.

The teams who built with me began to realize they had some major differences in how they defined the key systems and expectations of the team. They had a unique way of seeing the business that included structure and protocols. They had a mentality that included protecting their time and resources. They had a protocol that allowed them to enjoy and be present on a trip while most struggled to keep up with their business at home. Some attendees spent half of the trip on their cell phones. I was told they would ask others how they were possibly enjoying the trip so calmly and disconnected from their business without losing clients, deals, or their minds trying to keep the team at home on track.

You see, the people on their phones were islands occasionally visited by lifeboats. When the lifeboats came, they took the food and water, but not the fishing rods, water purification kits, or the seeds. Literally, they were the cog in the wheel, the checklist, and the knowledge. They were the source, the service, and the outcome of the business. They were the system, and everything else was band-aid solutions that helped but failed in delegating tasks away from the leader.

Now, I was not on this trip. Full transparency that I am sharing the perspective from those who called me after the trip frazzled, having spent a vacation on their phone while witnessing that others found a better way. The proof was right in front of their eyes. I am also sharing this perspective from what was shared with me by those who had phone-free time on this same trip and were now able to see how far they came now that they have help and real free time. They used to be the frazzled agent working on vacation, and now those very agents wanted to know how they were doing so much more business while spending less time working in the business.

There were a few other interesting aspects of the strategy calls I did after this trip. We had several individual producers, some with an assistant or administrative help, realizing that they spent a decade-plus building a top 1% business that would no longer be top 1% for very much longer. The gap was closing fast between frazzled, one-face business models and leaders who were doing a far lower level of personal sales production themselves and instead were spending more time coaching from the sidelines, assessing investment and profits from the owner's suite. The one side was building leaders on the field, and the other side was the only leader on the field representing their team.

The frazzled agents were surprised at the training and confidence of the teams that prepared their hires to maintain a specific protocol that they could all trust. Essentially, their teams all spoke the same language, had a clear and consistent playbook, and had the same steps to accomplish an outcome with a client, which gave their team leaders the confidence to sleep at night or travel with their clients in hands they trusted back at home. In a very real way, they established written and spoken terms of engagement that became the language of the team.

One of the calls that came in after that trip was from Maurice, who was struggling with the idea of a team. He clearly stated that he really did not want a team and resisted building one for a few years. Maurice valued client experience and was proud of the high level of insight he provided his clients. He was well-versed in many aspects of economics and investment and did not want to dilute his standards of service. What swayed him? Eventually, as Maurice watched and naturally analyzed his market, he noticed something. Others were teaming up and starting to offer expensive services in his market—expensive in terms of time to orchestrate and in money to produce. Whether it was marketing or client services, Maurice was seeing for himself that the shared revenue of a team would be the only way to continue to offer the best level of service and results in his market. Exactly what held him back from building a team became his number one reason to expand. He was leading by fire in the fight to offer more to the people he wanted to serve most.

I have worked with Maurice for several years now. One of the key things he did was build a compensation system to pay his sales team based on business principles versus the norm in his market. This allowed him to invest in the growth, opportunities, and security his clients and new team members needed for success. On future trips, Maurice would have notes to compare his team versus others, and eventually, he shared his team model, which allowed for higher profits and quicker growth. About a year and a half in, he more than doubled his business from 130 homes sold yearly to 260 over a twelve-month period. There were too many sales opportunities and not enough salespeople to take them. His support positions were rocking, and, once again, it was time to use the GENIUS Model to expand and stop doing tasks that limited the team's ability to provide better service during massive growth.

Sustaining Excellence as You Grow

The answer to creating the client experience you want will not likely be what you expect. You may expect unlicensed help taking over everything on day one, or sales help showing up at your door with clients in hand knowing exactly how to sell like you. You may attempt to have new hires shadow you as you go with the hopes your system will jump out at them more clearly, instead of the unique things you did because you were adapting to a particular client. For example, you may be outgoing and found it enjoyable to do extra small talk with a client, or maybe you offered a lower commission once but it's not something you do every time.

Here are a few things you can do to protect yourself as you hire:

Culture First

Explain what you believe in and why. This will shape everything you train and allow others to communicate a consistent message. What are your non-negotiables? How do they win and thrive with you? What should they not do, ever, as it would violate your values? What are you values?

Create a Bullseye

How do you win? What counts as success? You need to outline the desired outcome every step of the way. You also need to outline how to get there.

Hiring, Systems, and Training

Hiring is a process to identify the right candidate to accomplish a list of tasks. A system is how you do those tasks to create a predictable and consistent result. Creating systems and training simultaneously is messy, time-consuming, and exhausting. This is exactly why most people end up working more and selling less when they hire. They are trying to recreate the wheel and train at once, so they end up being on call for every question. This often lasts forever while they try to figure it all out.

Know Your Hand-Offs

Hiring help will challenge you in several ways. One of the best aspects of hiring is using the experience to test how organized you were before the hire. When you hire for unlicensed activities, you will need to slow down to get in the office or in front of the computer and document the steps that will be delegated to that hire. This can feel tedious, but remember, the hours you take to do these tasks yourself—if you do it right—will soon be removed from your plate on a weekly basis forever. This also creates an important base of value for other salespeople to join your business later. When you do hire for licensed sales, that new hire will test how well you did when you set up systems with the administrator. Did you create a universal system any sales agent could be trained on and benefit from? You need to know, when you pass the ball, who has it, what they will do with it, and if/when it is coming back.

Create a Better Experience

Why do some clients get A+ service and others get a D if they are lucky? How much do we spend on client gifts, and who gets one? Do some people get an invite to a client event while others do not? Anyone you hire is an extension of you. The goal is to create an elevated experience beyond the typical producer in your industry. Everyone under your business should get the same treatment, whether you bring in the clients or another team member brings them in. Everything you do is to strengthen the brand, client experience, and build the database. If you have different treatment for different clients, make it a system based on repeat business, price range, commission range, or what we call VIP COIs (meaning center of influence—people who are much more likely to refer you, repeat working with you, and/or influence others to work with you). Build a transparent system for how these people are treated or billed, but the goal is identical level of service and standards for all clients in each category.

Document Everything as You Go

Standard operating procedures, operations manuals, and/or training manuals are key. They can easily become a document collecting dust on a shelf, but they need to be a key ingredient to create confidence as you expand. Remember Sarah and Ben? Could you imagine someone leaving them again without them having everything documented to train the next hire? The pain of even contemplating exposing themselves to that type of risk again was too much. Often, we have to get burned before we understand the advice of those already wearing the wounds of business building. Document everything and update all changes. This is a non-negotiable. Make it a living, breathing document, and ensure training is always done around those documents.

I get it. Maybe you do not want to get more help. Maybe you do not like to manage others, or you feel they should be able to figure it all out like you did. I know you figured it out, and I would bet some of the people you hire will be able to figure it out too. But I need to ask you an important question: what do you want?

If you want a group where everyone is passing ships in the night, doing their own thing, and providing some basic relief, you can do that with less training and prep. Remember that those people, even in a group, are out representing your name. They are creating a new version of your reputation with the public every single day. Go to a party and mention a top team in the area. I recommend you do this as an experiment. Notice the names that repeatedly come up. Notice they do not bring up how well the team does, how many sales, all the happy clients. No, they bring up that one team member who gives everyone else a bad name.

All it takes for a team to fail is one team member who does not follow protocol, also known as having no interest in keeping the teams' commitments and promises to clients or the public. They do things their own way, and you thought you wanted that. You did not want to be too involved in their business. Now, they are delivering little to nothing in return for the costly opportunities and leads they demand of the business, and are costing you hard-earned dollars. They will start challenging you on the value of staying with the team, but what is the team doing for them?

Everything you do is an investment in the brand reputation and trust in the community. Would you invest in the same stock again and again without a return on investment or a loss? Most of you instantly said, "No." You would not continue to invest in a stock without a return if you were aware of its poor performance. Yet, we struggle to let go of team members who push us to give more without delivering a return for themselves or the business. That scenario is toxic for everyone, and it is contagious, so proceed with caution.

Your role is to protect and elevate your services, reputation, and brand. That is the dream, and anything that takes the team away from that dream does not just hurt you—it hurts your clients and it hurts the reputation that other team members rely on to build their business as well. It hurts the momentum and performance of your A players and deteriorates the status quo of what your business stands for. We will talk about performance culture later. Champions protect the whole. They live for the dream. Entitlement sucks the air out of the room. Even a champion struggles when they cannot breathe.

Chapter 8

STOP BABYSITTING! GET HELP
WITHOUT HIRING SALES AGENTS

Myth: *The people I hire "want to work for me."*

Truth: All sales agents were attracted to the industry because they didn't want to be employees. This is *the* dream. If you take away the dream, your team members will not stay long. Allow them and help them to build their business inside yours, and you will keep them forever.

I f you are looking to leverage with unlicensed help, then it's time to talk hiring. But if you are looking to bring in self-starting salespeople who will run with opportunities, aim for the bullseye, have a desire to excel, and make lots of money, then you will never want to "hire" again. We will talk about exactly why you do not want to hire for sales in a minute. Now, before we talk about why you do not want to hire for sales, let's talk about how to prepare to hire unlicensed non-sales support. This will allow you to free up your time as quickly as possible.

What the Heck Do I Do Now?

This is the most common question I get asked. I am hiring or recruiting, but what do I do? What does a team leader do?

This is "*the*" question!

The reality is that you need to hire yourself for your future role mentally first. For hiring your future self to your future position with the team, you will follow the first few steps of the hiring process below. Before envisioning your roles and responsibilities, remember that you are in the Mindset Matrix where everything becomes real for you. This means you are mentally shifting into multiple roles in your business already, far before you will fully transition into those future roles.

When James started working with me, he had two other team leaders in the mix. We quickly profiled all team leaders and assessed strengths. James was an ideal profile to build out the business as team leader. His Genius or G and E activities were in vision, strategy, systems, and implementation. The other team leaders were a mix of sales and management. This gave us the information we needed to understand the ideal fit to expand quickly with the people we had. We had strong leaders in sales to support the gross earnings of the team while James implemented steps to build out other income-producing roles and the systems to support them all. Each role was created with a specific goal of evening the scales between the number of sales coming from the team leaders and the number of sales coming from the new recruits. We needed to achieve this as soon as possible.

Balancing the scales is a huge tipping point in success for team building. The scales become even when the team matches the team leader in sales earnings or overall production. This is a very special point where we are off the ground and have a very real base to continue to grow the sales team and/or transition the team leader slightly away from sales and further into building and leading the business.

With multiple team leaders, we needed a strong strategy and a massive amount of trust. Everyone was investing their time, energy, and money to build the vision of a strong team where each leader and member could live operating in their GENIUS. We took the time to understand the vital areas where James, stepping into the role of Team Leader, always needed to have his finger on the pulse of the business.

This is a great moment to remember the different perspectives of business.

We had James and his two business partners in the owner's box. They were investing to build a business that would deliver returns and profits in the future with money, time, and energy.

We had the team leader at the side of the field working with me as the coach to train and maintain the results possible with our company playbook. We formulated a strategy that detailed what our big vision was and how we were going to get there. We knew that gaps between where we were now compared to our big vision. We knew our values, playbook, and by what means we would operate to reach our goal. We knew what our current players wanted, their skillset, who to put on the bench, who to take off the bench, how long to train each, and what to train them on. We knew who would receive company opportunities, and everyone knew how these opportunities would be distributed. Our performance expectations, pay levels, tracking, and accountability were all transparent. This initial analysis on expansion and how to build step-by-step allowed us to know where building this current step would allow us to build into the next step in the business. I recommend using the GENIUS Method and investing in team expansion models or proven organization charts, to review twice a year. This will allow you to forecast next steps as well. You need to know where you are and where you are going at all times.

Sales are on the field, face-to-face with other players trying to support the fans by bringing home the win. In this case, two of the owners were operating as sales while we recruited on others. This was a massive advantage to protect the team. This allowed for secure earnings as they built. Salespeople rely on the team leaders/coaches for the plays, to analyze the field, and to train them on where they need to go. Sales also relied on leadership to create the right mindset leading them into the future. This mindset, sales training, and environment will predict the future of production for each salesperson. On a strong team, the team leaders have a vested interest in the success of those players on the field. Could you imagine playing any level of competitive sports without a coach or leader? You are on the field to execute. Leadership is there to analyze the best strategy and give instructions for that execution, ensuring you are prepared well in advance.

Support positions are the doctors, physical therapists, assistant coaches, and others to keep the players in the game. They are there for two reasons only: to free up time by doing tasks which support the licensed sales reps to spend more time with clients, and to improve the client experience and the services offered to the public. At the end of the day, it will always come back to those two things. Even if you have a personal assistant to the team leader or a marketing role, it will still come down to supporting an ability to have more opportunities with an ever-elevating standard of services and experiences to clients.

James and his two business partners grew fast. They are a 20X success story. They expanded their business twenty times from where they were when they started to work with us. They built for where they were going with precision. They are one of those stories that go in books and magazines, but even with their swift implementation and commitment to create roles that they could continually leverage, it was still messy, difficult, and required extra hours for what I call "pinch seasons." Their growth required a phenomenal amount of persistent, determined dedication. It was not easy. They could have stopped when they had enough help to free up their time. They were already ahead. But that was not what they wanted. They built to have a foundation for expansion.

You may stop expanding your team after your first hire, if just having more time is exactly what you want. But let me ask you this. How can you know? How can you know what you will want until you are standing there? How can you know what the future will hold? I would wager a bet that you may surprise yourself and choose something different once you forced your way, building a path and coming to the next step to discover it is a fork in the road. How could you know which way you will go in the future until you are there? Until you reach a point when the next path presents itself in front of you?

Here is the thing. Pursuing this step, the goal of freeing up more time—this step is in front of you right now. Succeeding at this step affords you the ability to see the next potential step. I cannot know what you will do or want once you get there. I did not set out to have endless opportunities. Like you, I sought a sustainable life. Then, along the way, something changed, after so many, "If I could just get someone to help with billing, someone to help driving the kids when I am stuck elsewhere, someone to help with laundry for the busy months, someone to cut the grass, someone to be with clients when I take a vacation, someone to answer the phones, someone to help clients when I am with other clients, someone to create better marketing and visuals, someone to nurture people during follow-up when they are ready to sign up, someone to support the client in their process, and someone to ensure all of those people hear from us and know who we are…" I could go on all day.

I got addicted to leverage. I watched the same process unfold with James and countless other team leaders, as the "if onlys" were always followed by new ones. Why? Because when you live the GENIUS Method, you will train your brain to let go of what is heavy—the people, places, and things that no longer work for you. You will want to stop setting people up to need you in their piece of the process.

Think about it: If you hire, train, and nurture for Genius-level team members, your constant involvement is lowering your standards and results. Therefore, that is why we have the I for "Involve Others" on the GENIUS Model. Too many leaders get stuck "halfway leveraging." Involving others in your tasks versus empowering others in their Genius are very different things. Involving yourself in the role of others is adding to your roles of owner, team leader, salesperson, and now a piece of the job description for everyone you hire or recruit.

When you consider this buffet of roles, I want you to know the buffet was set out on the table for hours, and you are picking up the remnants left that no one wanted. This is not some beautiful feast when you are only ever cleaning up.

I want you to immediately imagine a disaster film filled with burnout, lost dreams, sadness, suffering, lost potential, and general defeat and failure. I have seen this film play out too many times, and I will not follow clients down this road anymore. It is too sad to watch. Please take the GENIUS Method and apply it. Sit down and enjoy your dinner. You are special, important, needed, and valuable, and you possess the gifts you are meant to bring to the world. You do not get there by standing back and cleaning up for everyone. You get there by empowering yourself and everyone else to stand in their role, thrive, finish and deliver. We have a lot less mess that way.

Spending your time in the wrong areas or on the wrong tasks costs you pennies in energy. I want you to envision 100 pennies a day. That is all you get. They are on an electronic swipe card with no room for extra credits. You get on that subway, spend the fare, or you don't—that's it. Would you get on your team member's subway cart to watch them drive? Maybe. It might give you some confidence to see their driving skills at the beginning for sure, but later, every time you get on their subway car to watch them drive, your own subway train is now lacking a driver and could potentially de-rail. You cannot be two places at one time, but your skills and standards can.

The point is, drive yourself. Leadership is all about leading yourself first. We spend so much time trying to lead others. The world and our business are better off with humans who lead themselves one glass castle shattered at a time.

In the end, none of us know what we will want in the future. My job is to ensure you have choices. If you get help and want to stay in that position, great. But what if you get help and like the look of the new path presented, and you see a waterfall ahead on the detour, which leads to a lookout point, which leads to a clear view of the horizon, which leads to a path to the emerald grotto reflecting green sunshine kissed water with a jewel like glow? If you see that first detour and it feels tempting, I hope you go. I hope you take the path of growth when it is presented to you. For that reason alone, if only to satisfy the "what if" statement, I will ensure any steps we take together lead you to an ability to choose other paths, to take other detours, and to grow even more if you wish.

KBCC Ultimate Leadership Focus Matrix

All the leaders who freed up their time used a version of this process to have clarity on their role during expansion. This is what James used to keep his finger on the pulse of the business as it grew. You will want to understand these five facets and how they will arm you for greater success every time you expand.

There is only one way to go up, and that is on solid ground. Everything else is simply a ride at the amusement park. You can start off strong and swift, but you always end up right back where you started with a swift jerk as someone forces the brakes for you, not with you. Anyone building a business was on that ride. We know how it feels, and, for most of us, we will accidentally board again as we attempt to find the actual path to the peak of the mountain. Tip: The real thing is not automated, nor driven and energized by someone else. The real solution is getting highly intimate with your role and the key facets of your business. That is where the Leadership Focus Matrix will become invaluable to you.

Vision

Vision is your best way to bend reality while living in the mindset of the expansion Matrix. Vision gives you depth. Make decisions on where you will be in the business in two to five or ten years. Literally envision the business as it *will be* and decide from that place. This clears the clutter and allows you to be in it for the business first. Strong cultures thrive with a unified vision that works for the whole. Decide based on where you are going, not where you are.

Opportunity

Can you create additional client opportunities? Can you fill the hours you are freeing up for yourself with a mix of new clients and personal time? Do you have enough client opportunities to support new sales positions? The team leader is responsible for being in tune with the opportunities the business needs. This includes anticipating opportunities based on the fluctuations of the business—watching metrics for leads, clients, contracts, and firm deals in real-time while forecasting upcoming results in the next sixty to ninety days for the team.

Performance Culture

Are you training to prepare yourself and, later, any sales recruits to thrive in the opportunities you have? What do team members need to know before they are handed valuable opportunities? Team members may want and demand opportunities, and it is up to you to prepare them for success and ensure a high likelihood of return for the business. Performance cultures are not built for comfort. We need to invest in the training systems, environment, mindset, accountability, and the GENIUS Method to create a platform delivering consistent, predictable results. We need to be willing to take action to get back to results quickly.

Team Growth

You will want to have urgent ninety-day focus points for the team. This is vital to ensure you are always moving back on track. In my experience, this is a constant course current. No one is "on-track" all the time but rather living in the awareness of what is required and taking action to get back on track.

You need to know who you have now on the team, note any urgent changes, as well as what Genius is needed next in the future. If you are visual, do an organizational chart or simply type the roles and tasks, currently and twelve to eighteen months in the future.

How are you nurturing current team members? Who are you bringing on the team and what additional opportunities will they allow for the business? What is your process to identify your needs, top talent, and welcome the best candidates to your team?

ROI

This is the area most team leaders do not love. Remember, you can delegate and leverage out all five areas of expansion listed here, but you must keep yourself informed with the metrics, goals, strategies, and struggles of those key areas. This is vital to your expansion.

Why would ROI be a less-liked area? It involves tracking, accountability, budgets, profit and loss statements; and overall, a good, honest dose of what cold air feels like when rushing into a warm room. Most people do not run toward that reality. A task-oriented mind is excited and filled with joy to see a dashboard indicating metrics to show that you are successfully getting more "on-track" toward a larger goal. If you cringe at the idea of tracking and metrics overall, you need a coach, strong team support person, or manager to bring you the information as you train yourself on what to look for, what to do about it, and why. For many of you, a team manager may be outside the budget, and an initial administrator/unlicensed assistant will be busy in their role and may not have the expertise to support you. A coach with the expertise to stand in the cold air and help you with strategic solutions will be vital.

The KBCC Ultimate Leadership Focus Matrix is an ever-continuing tool with a flow from the top of the list to the bottom of the list as you continue to grow the business. This will ensure you get stronger every time you expand your vision or goals in the business. You will get closer and closer to your five- and ten-year goals, as that is the place your decision making now lives. You will be creating ever-expanding opportunities. You will invest in the best way to serve those opportunities to create results. You will nurture the help you have and only grow the team with the right GENIUS to support the business. Later, you will ensure a thriving client experience by giving opportunities based on a team member's ability to create experiences that lead to results. These measured results will reflect a team members ability to successfully bringing your values, standards, and services to the public. You will know this is the case because you are connected. You have your finger on the pulse of tracking. You know how to pay others, invest in growth, pay yourself, and profit to ensure a healthy business.

KBCC Ultimate Hiring System

We worked with hundreds of teams and thousands of salespeople to hire effectively. This system delivered hundreds of interested applicants. However, the key is working the system to help you identify the right GENIUS to support you, ensure they can work on their tasks without needing you, and free up your time.

You will find spending more time on Step 1 leads to clarity, and clarity leads to conscious choices. Envision exactly what you want; envision the ideal candidate—describe them, include their imminent arrival in your everyday discussions, plan for them before they arrive. Not only will this prepare you to act, but this will also make it easier for the existing team to support and prepare for the new hire. Remember that your support roles will thrive on consistency. This helps everyone see the new hire before they are physically present.

Step 1: Job Description

- What do you need this hire to do? List all tasks and expectations for this role.
- What does a win look like?
- What would you *not* want to see?
- How does this role create additional momentum for you and the business?

- Does this role make the company money by freeing up time for additional clients or by bringing additional clients into the business?
  - What is the ideal personality type to thrive with the tasks listed?
  - Do you need someone task-oriented, social, friendly, fast-paced, precision-paced, detail-oriented, bottom line-oriented, support-oriented, people-oriented, someone who will speak up, someone who will nurture?
  - What personality assessment is best for you to find a match between the candidate you need and the candidate applying?
  - Who is trained to support you in creating the profile and assessing candidates? Do you have a coach, a team member, or a team leader, certified in personality assessments?
  - Who is this person? Describe them. What is this person's name? What does this person do for fun? Why is this person interested in this position, and what will make this person apply, accept, and stay in this position?

You have an extra edge on this job description because you already completed your GENIUS Model to identify exactly what tasks you need to leverage next and what leveraging is worth to the business in time and money. But remember, you are not doing this from your perspective. You are not the ideal person for this role. If you were the ideal person, these tasks would not be identified as N, I, U, or S tasks in your GENIUS Model. It is time to free yourself from the expectation that you must be good at everything or that others need to see the world the way you do. Others do not see the world the way you do, and that is what makes teams work. Partner with GENIUS, cast a vision, train, maintain culture and accountability, and get the heck out of the way!

Step 2: Create an Enticing Ad

This is where you describe the dream. What is the overall opportunity available to the person who is selected for this position? You might include existing skills and experience if you are looking for someone in-tune with their GENIUS, or you may cast a vision for what you want. If you cast a vision for what you want, be prepared to use this system to identify talent and potential GENIUS, but you will be responsible for training this person on skills, systems, and expectations. This will usually be a lower pay rate for the business. Another reason a business will invest in potential talent is to maintain a process that they know works. For example, James implemented the database and administrative systems for my team. We knew what we wanted to build, we had the playbook, and we wanted to avoid having to reset habits outside of our vision. We also knew that the playbook we had included steps for the future, and those steps required Level 1 to be done a certain way; otherwise, Level 2 would not work.

Cast a vision for the full opportunity with any perks that the right candidate you described in Step 1 would value. Things like flex time, work from home, paid vacation, sick days, training opportunities, and future expansion from part-time to full-time or hours around school times. You want to offer the net value of an annual package. It is not just about the money.

Step 3: Online Response

Your ad should entice the right people and make them want to learn more. Your ad will also entice the wrong people who will waste a lot of your time, so you want to prevent that from happening. Time is something you cannot spare; therefore, you do not want to spend a lot of time on this step. Leverage technology to help you sift through the ad responses before you get too involved. Remember, if this is your first hire, this will be a pinch season for you, meaning you need to keep sales up. Using this system will save you a massive amount of time until you have the help you need to do this for you in the future.

You want to create a reply with some of the key tasks on your job description. Provide a personality assessment and request your candidates to complete it and return it to you with a skills test or task to complete. Also, request a resume and have your candidates indicate a salary range. Give a deadline to complete this step.

You can create an autoresponder that sends this step to anyone who replies to your ad. This will save you even more time and leave you only needing to open the emails that are directly replying to this second step in the process.

Do not waste your time. If a candidate is not willing to complete a personality profile and skills test or send a resume, you have one of two things happening. This is either a massive success, because you now know this person is not that interested and saved you both a lot of time; or you are not offering a vision that entices the right people with either your ad, online response, or both. Go back to Step 1, and keep in mind that this is relative. Are you looking for a unicorn? Great! Most people want to feel unique and special, so refine your ad to speak to your unicorn directly. If about 25% of the initial ad replies are now sending the online response, it is working. Move on to Step 4.

Step 4: Phone Interview

Review applicants who replied against the description in Step 1. Compare the personality assessment they completed to the ideal profile you created with a personality profiling expert. Review the resume for relevant experience, if needed. Remember, you only need to hire one person. You do not need to speak to everyone. Only select your top applicants for phone interviews. If they did not complete the personality profile, skills test, or resume requirement, they are out of the process. Put those applicants to the side.

Set a block of time for phone interviews that work for you. Congratulate the top ten candidates by offering them one of the

15-minute spots for a phone interview. If possible, have a lunchtime or late afternoon time block. Your ideal candidate may already be employed, and you want to talk to them!

Be prepared with a list of questions. Ask open-ended and situational questions. Listen to how they process, what they value, and what are they are willing to use their personal resources toward—think time, money, energy, and focus.

- What is most important to them about working with a team?
- What is most important to them about their workplace?
- What goals do they have for the next year? What about two years? Five years?
- What makes them happy?
- What was the last book they read?
- Favourite movie?

Be willing to cut the interview short if there are obvious issues with communication or answers that clearly indicate the candidate will not thrive in the role. Be most willing, open, and able to use the ultimate leadership skill: *Look for GENIUS in others, even when they may not yet see it.* Great recruiters build leaders up; they cast a vision in the applicants' eyes and elevate them into a position just as much, or more than, they attract and place them.

Now is the tricky part. You want to narrow the top phone interviews based on all the information you have so far down to three to five candidates maximum to move on to Step 5.

Step 5: In-Person Interview

Be prepared with questions ahead of time. You want to duplicate some of the questions you used during the phone interview. Listen for consistency between the two interviews.

- What are they passionate about?
- Why should we choose them?
- What would they love to work on as a project if they were chosen for this position?
- Do they have a bucket list?
- What is their top bucket list goal?
- Do they prefer to work with people or technology?
- Would they rather complete a task fast or accurately?
- What was the most difficult situation in a workplace and what did they learn?
- Dan Sullivan from Strategic Coach uses a specific question to assess a match with millennials within his company. He asks, "If you are chosen, what are you entitled to in this position?"

Take notes. If you have an existing team member, have that team member attend also and take notes.

Watch for punctuality, attire, confidence, and communication skills. Nerves are normal; however, an inability to answer questions or elaborate on answers is a red flag. We already established that you probably have a busy business that will require someone strong who can think on their feet, follow a process, and deal with clients and the public on your behalf. An inability to communicate in a stressful situation is likely to cause issues for you in the business later.

Step 6: Secret Weapon

You can use a secret weapon to bring the top GENIUS to your attention for one of two reasons. If you still have several applicants in the running and you cannot decide, or if you are not 100% sure about anyone, you can send a simple assignment.

Give the applicant 24 hours to reply to either a set of questions and/or a project that would emulate the work they would do with your team. If you choose the questions, the whole point is to give some creative liberty to applicants to show you who they really are and what they are most excited about when they think about joining your team. Allow them to use any medium they would like to reply—video, art, poetry, musical, and writing are all fair game. Leave it up to them to choose what they communicate and how they communicate it. This will show you a lot about the person.

If you choose a project, create something that would be like a task you would assign. Set expectations and a timeline. For example, a social media graphic and copy or an email to past clients. Sky's the limit! Struggling with something in your business right now and want to assess the applicant's GENIUS? Assign them the task and see what they come up with. This should be reasonable and take up to an hour or two of work maximum. Reserve this for legitimate finalists in the hiring process.

Step 7: Working Interview/Training

You have now used the KBCC Ultimate Hiring System to bring the top candidate to the surface. Offer them to begin training as working interview or offer them the position. If you are still stuck between two candidates, a working interview is essentially a start to training and observing how well each candidate picks up on and retains what you need in the business.

It is probably obvious, but you are at a disadvantage here if you do not have systems to train them on. I know you are busy, but this is where you may want help to access the tools, systems, and processes you may need in the business from someone who already has them. Start with the tasks that you need to take off your plate to free up now. After you have moved some of the essentials to your new hire, you may want to leverage to your advantage.

If the company that has this content also offers training support, you will want to seriously consider this option. You know how much your time is worth. Creating systems and training someone on them at the same time is messy, time-consuming, and costs you a lot of money. But when the business needs something, you have to find the GENIUS to deliver it. It does not have to be you. In fact, it would probably cost the business more initially for you to do this step.

Step 8: Hold and Increase Your Earnings

Remember the commitment you made to how many hours you were going to use in the business versus personal time when you brought on help? Stick to that commitment. You wanted to leverage more time and more money. By reinvesting the hours, you free up time for additional sales opportunities that will allow you to accomplish this goal.

If you do not have enough extra sales opportunities, use this extra time to focus on prospecting existing leads in your database. First, clean up past dropped opportunities. You'll usually strike gold if you keep notes. Let your new team members help with some easy ways to bring the low-hanging fruit to your attention. Search for Dean Jackson's 9-word email on Google. Start there to see who is still interested. This will allow you to get some new opportunities while you get cleaned up and organized enough to cultivate your leads properly in the future. Once that is done, spend the time on marketing and lead generation. Not having face-to-face opportunities in front of you does not count as extra personal time; it means you are responsible to create those extra opportunities.

Recruitment Versus Hiring

Risk is worth something. Your risk to build a business. To invest, to profit, to face a loss, to potentially borrow against personal or business credit to float the business, to hold the future of a business and its members in your hands—that involves risk, and once you get some time back, you should get paid extra for that risk. For you, the risk of continuing to live a life without time—time to carve out the next step with the business; time to enjoy family and friends; time to take care of yourself physically, mentally, and emotionally—the risk of continuing to live without time is greater than the risk to expand. We covered the actual risk and rewards for you to get help as a team leader and business owner. For the person you will "hire", the risk is a lack of security. For the person you "recruit", the risk is a lack of opportunity.

Focus on the overall value package your team can offer to a potential recruit. Just like you did in Step 1 of the KBCC Ultimate Hiring Process, you will want to envision the ideal agent to represent your name, your brand, and your reputation. Envision their ideal personality, personal attributes, dreams, and goals. Envision the problems they are facing in trying to grow their business on their own. Identify the issues potential team members have faced joining other teams. What gave the team a bad name in your area? Why don't salespeople want to join a team? Flip those problems and frustrations into solutions. Meet your potential recruits where they are by trying to solve their immediate problems and provide the opportunities they need.

For example, most agents hate prospecting, paperwork, and lead generation. Would a typical agent be interested in an opportunity where they never had to cold call, pay for marketing, or do administrative tasks?

Sales is a hard position. Most people fail. Most people leave the role or industry altogether. In real estate, 80% of new agents who obtain a license will leave or do next to no business within eighteen months. Commission sales as an income or career is not for everyone; and yet, some people excel quickly in the industry.

If you could take away the problems, offer support, experience, training, and take away the tasks that agents typically dislike, what would it be worth to them? What is it worth to you?

You want to take the best possible year in value, training, net income, results, and time that ideal candidates could achieve if they fully applied themselves and did what you taught them. This includes using the approach you will teach them to achieve the results of your best sales agent. That is the dream. You cast the dream that the independent sales driver seeks. You do not take responsibility for their side of the coin. You do not guarantee their results. You guarantee the opportunity. You guarantee delivery of the opportunities and approach they can use to bring that dream to fruition for themselves using your help and platform. You offer the full package—the net value of working with the team on an annual basis. Money is only a piece of that value package. Good people leave teams that pay them a lot, even too much, to handle parts of the business they do every day. But, great people will stay on teams with more modest pay for their entire careers. Why is this? Because great people are motivated to do great work with great people! We need opportunity, security, powerful projects, community, performance culture, and compensation to retain great people. Overpaying ties our hands to create and invest in these vital aspects that actual keep great people wanting to be on our teams.

Compensation is just the beginning. Compensation is not even close to everything that attracts, nurtures, and retains the right people to thrive with your team. You need to make enough money to be comfortable enough to look up toward what matters to you most. What matters most is different for everyone, but almost always contains the theme of worthwhile work; personal meaning;

an understanding that what you do matters; and a contribution to a cause, goal, or vision much bigger than one's self.

Start with net value at the end of the year. This net value represents a combination of compensation, security, and opportunity. Get compensation off the table. You want your team members to knock compensation off as a primary focus. Remember, drivers often drive in pursuit of safety and control from experiences of lack in their lives. This means security is important to everyone on the team. Help team members to have enough value within the team so that they can safely move their focus to fulfillment, knowledge acquisition, and powerful projects. Know more, give more, make more.

Chapter 9
AVOIDING COMMON
AND COSTLY MISTAKES

Myth: *If I pay my team members more, I am a better team leader.*

Truth: The team leader's purpose is to offer value, not the best split or pay. Value is communicated in terms of systems, support, an abundance of leads, appointments, education and training, and opportunities for growth. Net money means that your agents buy into the bigger picture of more leads, more deals, more support, and more systems, ultimately leading to much more money for all.

After coaching hundreds of real estate teams full-time since 2009, I knew when I started Kathleen Black Coaching &

Consulting Inc. (KBCC), that I wanted to continue my focus on team development and mindset. I believe in the power of team environments, and know that when done well, a team can put all the top characteristics associated with success into play prior to a new member joining. In fact, the success of a new member has more to do with the team environment than the member him or herself.

Through my experience coaching teams, I found three reoccurring difficulties facing team leaders as they work toward expanding their business: compensation, training, and recruitment. They aren't entire roadblocks, as most team leaders who stumble to grow become more open to the solutions they resisted in the first place. Often, if you are the type of leader who needs to try what you think will work first, regardless of if it failed 100% of the time in my team's experience, then the best thing to do is go for it and hope that it is going to fail and fail fast so we can get on track.

For every problem, there is a solution. I write articles, present webinars, and even frame events around the most common obstacles facing a team leader. You need to ensure you have the information you need to build smart from the start or to rebuild smart when you need to. With the dismal rate of success for those attempting to build a sales team, I recommend you know what to look for and how to solve these three common issues upfront.

Compensation Structure

After making the transition from a top-producing realtor on a top-producing team to running a team-specific coaching company,

I was able to pinpoint the first and most prominent of the three mistakes made by team leaders as the compensation structure. As you'll recall, a lot of team leaders do not set themselves up to be compensated for their new role as team leader. A lack of compensation for that role creates a broken equation where the team leader returns his or her focus to sales instead of working to grow the team business and nurture the people on the team.

I like to emphasize the need for a connection between building the business and being compensated for the role of team leader. It is essential for the team leader to see the value in being the leader. The team leader has a vital role on the team, and that comes with a job description and tasks. Remember, you hire yourself for this promotion first. No one else is going to ensure you do it right to protect yourself and your investment for the future. Most team leaders are floating the entire business on their personal sales. This approach will lead to frustration. Team leaders need to recognize the need to compensate themselves accordingly.

In determining what works best as a compensation structure, I want to reinforce the idea of compensating for your value, what you bring to your team, as well as considering the future of the team. With KBCC coaching clients, my team and I evaluate every influencing factor when approaching the compensation structure, but what makes the custom compensation structures so effective is that it is always targeted toward the goal of where the team will be in the future instead of where the team is currently. Ten years down the road, the team will not be composed of the team leader and one team member, so capping at a 50/50 split is extremely restrictive.

I always recommend taking into account the vision. If your team will have a lead conversion partner and a licensed assistant or a manager that will allow all salespeople to benefit from increasing leverage on the team, then you need to prepare for that from the beginning. If you do not see the need to expand beyond unlicensed support and potentially one sales role, at least keep your options open. Build a structure that will give you choices later. Remember that path that may present itself once you get where you are going. You want to give yourself the ability to take other paths later.

I also want to remind you to account for a team's expenses, such as marketing, overhead, and any additional costs that the team carries. You spent the time to move into the Mindset Matrix of a business owner. Remember, a business owner looks at net income and profits. The team produces a full amount as a business, regardless of if you are face-to-face with a client or another sales agent. Your face-to-face time has a value in a sales role. This way, considering all earnings and all expenses, the team has the resources to continue to grow and build, which is in the best interest of everyone involved. No one wants to build their business on the foundation of quicksand—not you, not your support team, and not your future salespeople. A strong business model benefits everyone on the team.

Training

The second difficult obstacle that team leaders face when building a team is training. A top producer doesn't necessarily make a top trainer. I identified with that personally from when I first made the change to be a coach. I did find a way around this challenge with the implementation of many training certifications and systems. In our industry, we have this idea that those selling the most should train and coach. In the team world, those with the area of Genius needed to propel us, should train, coach, and be leveraged. We have implemented DISC Personality Profiling Certifications for all of our coaches. I am a DISC Trainers' Trainer, a Master NLP Practitioner, an NLP Coach, an ABNLP certified in hypnotherapy, in addition to having an honours degree in psychology. I have invested in conflict management, personal development, energy mapping, all in addition to being an expert on my team's expansion model. Genius without communication or the ability to adapt to varying clients does not work.

When training, shadowing is generally the path taken when showing someone the ropes, but the mistake here is that every person does it differently every single time. This inconsistency doesn't work to effectively prepare an agent for success when that agent is on his own.

The team leaders that I coach work on the idea of mastery—everyone follows the same steps, so everyone knows what it takes to be successful. At that point, the agents approach the situations with their own personalities and interpretations, but they have been empowered with a set system to be successful.

When it comes to enforcing the training, anyone who talked to me about it knows this will be my answer: "Know it so well you can't forget it," so learning it all with intensive training and weeks dedicated to the art, ultimately, pays off more than any other implementation of the systems. Working with the KBCC model, you move beyond learning and memorization to having it become part of who you are. The effectiveness of this strategy is reflected in learning it once and never having to think about it again. This comes back to the idea of being empowered to be successful.

Training is a vital aspect of the KBCC Expansion Strategy for a reason. Having an agent trained and prepared prior to receiving opportunities is vital. Think of the average commission paid out in your business. What is that worth? What does it then cost you to put opportunities in the hands of unprepared salespeople? What does it cost them? I can assure you that it costs them far more than one commission cheque. Bad habits are repeatedly reinforced until we are immersed in a new way, and even then, it requires a lot of accountability to maintain new habits. Our brains like routine and repetition. Training a new approach is easiest at the start of joining a team, where the environment will be associated with certain values and systems for how you accomplish tasks.

Recruitment Systems

Recruitment, or lack of recruitment systems, is the third major obstacle faced by team leaders. The lack of recruitment systems has team leaders not looking into the business they want ten years down the road and recruiting people who ultimately don't complement the direction they want to take their team. One common example of this is taking someone on who is easy and comfortable. There won't be a push from them to help to achieve the levels of success that the team leader envisioned. With a lack of recruitment steps, most teams are missing the most important aspect of attracting new salespeople to the team: the dream!

Remember, you envisioned the ideal recruit and identified why you are recruiting with sales versus hiring. With recruitment, you are attracting others who want the freedom to build and operate their own business. Like you, they have certain areas of GENIUS and other areas costing them time and money. The foundation you are building to free up your time will do the same for others. You want to advertise what is possible with a full net value package. This package includes solving current problems and frustrations, making enough money, support, and opportunities. Money is part of the package, but not all of it.

When potential sales recruits reply to the ad, you want to cast the vision and dream from their perspective. You want them to see what is possible if they, too, partnered with GENIUS to focus on what they love in the business more and what drained their time and energy less. You want them to see themselves as part of your team. You want to encourage them to apply to assess a fit. You are looking for your ideal candidate. You are looking for candidates worth investing in for their growth and the growth of the team.

When looking at recruiting, a team leader isn't just faced with a few interested candidates. They're faced with the decision to invest what we equate to $20,000 to $25,000 of training into someone with no guarantee in return on that investment. Though there is no perfect equation for selecting the ideal future team members, I do think that you can get close if you use the right filters and steps for hiring and recruitment. When your clients look to recruit, depending on the size of the team, recruitment could be done monthly or as required. You will start with a DISC personality profile review, because team leaders need someone who both upholds the team's standards and values and can contribute to the team's continued drive to succeed. That is by no means the last step, but with further tests and questionnaires as part of your process, it is a telling starting point.

Ultimately, I encourage team leaders in any stage of growth to keep in mind these common mistakes. Each one of these avoidable team mistakes cost an incredible amount of money, time, effort, and frustration. When faced with expanding your team, often what seems logical or to make the most sense can be taking steps backward. Teams are unique and require a unique perspective around what works for top 1% teams. If you want to skip unnecessary mistakes, then you want to model the best and forget the rest. The best way to skip the pitfalls of average is to align yourself with the best and invest in access to their team-building strategy, systems, and expansion levels. We know how uncommon top 1% team-building advice is. You may get a few breadcrumbs, but breadcrumbs don't equate to a full loaf. You need all the pieces to build a strong congruent team foundation. You need all the pieces to build a foundation that gives you the confidence to invest and expand. Economic models built on business principles will always consider the compensation structure of those in sales, support, leadership, and ownership. These same principles are vital to protect you as you put reliable help in place. This advice applies whether you are a team of two to three or a team of fifty, seventy-five, or 100 plus.

With the compensation structure and knowing your worth as a team leader, training, implementing systems, and recruitment, you want to know upfront the direction you want to take or invest in a proven approach to avoid cement ceilings later. Otherwise, the best-laid plans will sabotage your growth in the future.

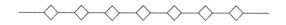

Chapter 10

HOW TO CREATE A
PERFORMANCE CULTURE

Myth: *Teams are profitable.*

Truth: Most teams are *not profitable*!

A healthy commission and compensation structure must consider three main things: make money for the team member, make money for the team leader, and make profits for the sustainability and growth of the team as a whole. All three of these things must be considered for there to be a win-win. Profits are arguably the most important here. They are also the most neglected. Profits are essential to ensure that you reinvest in the business, continue to grow, and offer some shelter in slower times. Let's be clear. If the business does not survive, thrive, and grow, it doesn't matter the agents' split or how much the team leader makes.

I cringe starting a chapter on performance with profit. Everything that makes me love team, performance, and the growth that all that allows relies on making enough money to support an ecosystem that is no longer focused on profit. Profit is not a purpose. Purpose is the reason we do the work. Profit is the indicator that the work we did brought value to the world. Profit and prosperity are the byproducts of a healthy purpose that made an impact.

Teams thrive on a sense of purpose, just like solo humans do. Purpose can create growth so transcendent that it changes the world. Purpose that is of a world-changing magnitude offers value and evolution to massive communities, either directly or indirectly, and that type of growth creates so many different types of prosperity. Prosperity can be opportunity, time, health, energy, clarity, and/or money, which make an increasing impact in your community, in the families of your team members, and the families of the clients you support. It has a ripple effect out to the world.

Prosperity is not the goal. A business capable of doing what you need it to do to have the life you want is the goal. Prosperity is the indicator that what you have and are building is working.

The reality is that you do not get off the ground building a team without some sweat equity, or what I call "pinch months." In the beginning, you invest your sweat and tears, and work smart to build and sell so you can create extra time, income, and profit. You can't hustle a business into existence with your bare hands forever, nor should you. But you will need to work with what you have until you create more. Then, you will work with what you have again, only now you will have more, and the direction on how to use your resources to grow faster. Build your route to GENIUS as quickly as possible, because if you don't, you will not get to witness the growth and evolution of team members into their next potential selves. You will not get to elevate your levels of service or your support into the community. None of this happens without a business that works, and simply put, a business that works in today's world includes profit.

Profit is one aspect of prosperity. Others include time, energy, inspiration, opportunity, focus, GENIUS, and the overall health of the people involved in your business and life.

If you recruit sales team members who do not work in their GENIUS to help people, your team will not work. A performance environment is vital to create, support, and nurture capability, leading to results for your business. Performance on a team is not optional. Without the components in this chapter, you do not have a team. You may have a group leveraging some resources, but you do not have the power of synergy or the full ability to leverage GENIUS among each other. Teams are interconnected in an expanding web of GENIUS and leverage. As Nick Sonnenberg says, "Complexity is exponential with team size." This complexity is a web of growing micro-steps, tasks, and support that moves across various members to align the team. Team systems are synergistic, whereas group systems are one solo user connecting directly for a shared service or delegation to serve their business.

For example, a group could be a one-time invite to practice with the rowing team. You get to have the experience. The team members of the rowing team practice together, train together, and have accountability for raising the team up with what they think, say, and do; or, alternatively, hold the consequences for anything that could be bringing the team down. With the rowing team, the goals of the team are the focus and the hub of all interactions. With the one-time invite to be part of the group, your focus is yourself—what you can learn and benefit—not the whole. The team provides a greater whole, whereas the group provides direct delegation for each person separately. The group lacks synergy, a cohesive environment, and almost always lacks the performance level of a team. The house always wins. A team has a house, and we all live there when working and sometimes when not working. It's a more influential house than you will ever build on our own. The environment always wins. We are products of our environments until we choose to change them.

The team requires a change of course and can pivot together almost instantly. The group is still trying to organize communication and compliance with their members while the team is already in motion. The group is constantly trying to figure out custom ways to do everyday tasks; everyone has a say—they could be collaborative—but who is responsible for bringing the level of expectation that will deliver what is best for all members? In sales, results are firm deals, and a team environment based on supporting performance will always deliver a higher number of happy clients and firm deals.

What Is a High-Performance Team?

"An interdependent, stable, role-defined group of individuals who share responsibility, mutual trust, and values, while having strong leadership, and a clear focus on a common goal."

The Performance Matrix

There are five factors that will contribute to a performance environment where team members have autonomy and personal accountability to get a project done, versus getting stuck and involved where you wanted to leverage. When you need to be involved, you reduce the room for team members to be responsible and you reduce their capability without your assistance. Your role as a leader is to build the components that lead to results, ensure your systems empower others to deliver the standards of your business, and hold team members accountable to keep the system on track. Manage the system and motivate the people. Let your people manage themselves once they are trained. Give them the room to have the dream that brought them into a sales role in the first place, which is to run their own business.

You want to go from surviving to thriving, and to do that, you need the secrets of high performing, collaborative teams. The five factors that are essential for leaders to create autonomous and accountable team members are ETMAG: Environment, Training, Mindset, Accountability, and GENIUS. They are what strong performance cultures are made of. Add in the core of passion, purpose, and power, and now you have the heart and soul of a performance culture. Let's break these main five areas down together.

Environment

> *"Culture, real culture, is radical and transformative"*
> **—Chris Hedge**

> *"When Culture and Strategy are not aligned ... Culture eats strategy for breakfast"*
> **—Peter Drucker**

> *"A human being is not one thing among others; things determine each other, but man is ultimately self-determining. What he becomes—within the limits of endowment*

and environment—he has made out of himself. In the concentration camps, for example, in this living laboratory and on this testing ground, we watched and witnessed some of our comrades behave like swine while others behaved like saints. Man has both potentialities within himself; which one is actualized depends on decisions but not on conditions."
—**Viktor E. Frankl**, Man's Search for Meaning

Your team environment is like the air you breathe. You often do not think about breathing at all throughout our day. You fail to notice when your chest constricts, or when you relax by the water breathing deeper into your stomach, or when your breath becomes shallow, and when you are breathing too fast. Top performers meditate to bring breath into their conscious awareness. We can manage our states by consciously altering our breath, and we are able to connect with others by moving closer to their breathing patterns as well. Our breath sets a pace, and that pace impacts our thinking, actions, and eventually, results.

A team environment is the unconscious breath you often do not pay attention to. You struggle when hires or sales recruits do not perform, but often the most obvious reasons are already surrounding you. A team operating together essentially creates an extra person or dynamic always in the office with you—that person represents the combination of everyone. That person has beliefs and standards that define everything that happens on the team. When left to its own devices, a team can be full of dysfunctions.

I recommend you read *The Five Dysfunctions of a Team* by Patrick Lencioni. In it, he explores the absence of trust, fear of conflict, lack of commitment, avoidance of accountability, and inattention to results as the main dysfunctions of a team. Lencioni also provides how to overcome these dysfunctions: be human, demand debate, focus on clarity and closure, confront difficult issues, and focus on outcomes. Lencioni is trying to describe the untouchables in a team and the aspects that surround, corrupt, and elevate us, but that are often grey, messy, and hard to navigate. The soft skills make a team, just like emotional intelligence makes a leader.

Part of your environment is a team identity. You need to establish the team's current mission, the future dreams of the team with a vision, and the values that guide the team. The values represent how you get there and include the standards and principles of your team. Values impact belief, which leads your train of thought in one direction or another, and beliefs later sift and sort information to justify what you already decided to do. Beliefs will dictate whether the person in the concentration camp, as Viktor E. Frankl described above, will behave as a swine or a saint in the direst of conditions. His point was that values or beliefs decide how we react to any situation, not the situation itself. We live what we believe. Values are powerful in that they direct and nurture our beliefs. Our values carve the map, whereas the vision is the North Star.

Team values are nurtured into performance as we bring them into the room and make them conscious and visible together. Team values represent everyone on the team and define the inclusive and exclusive elements of your culture. For example, teams thrive in the exclusive ways in which they approach the market, consumers, clients, and other members of the team. Teams thrive in the unique synergy that a hyper-focused, unified approach with a shared desired outcome or bullseye can deliver. On the other hand, inclusivity is important to grow and allow other people to penetrate the nucleus that is the in-crowd on your team. Everyone should be included in the in-crowd. If new members cannot merge with existing members, you will cap your growth, whereas a recruit that just does not believe what you do and, even with training, does not seem to fit in will be worked out of the team with hundreds of small reminders a day of how they do not belong. You want a culture exclusive enough to give you an edge and inclusive enough to attract great people, grow, and thrive together.

The key is to take the values from unconscious to conscious. In an unconscious team, scarcity may be ruling the show. You may believe that you have to be cutthroat to get a deal done. You may identify with hardcore, pushy, and manipulative tactics to get a sale. This is often apparent in every decision you make, but it is not empowering the team. A scarcity environment will forever leave salespeople behind seeking external validation for being a productive and capable salesperson based on transactions. Every agent is pitted against the next in an external and vicious cycle. In this scarcity environment, there is not enough business for everyone; and your team may win, but if you do, you'll win by taking from outside competition. A scarcity environment is based on comparison.

On the other hand, you could thrive in an abundance culture. Abundance is deliberate, conscious, and a joyous surrender. We do not compare in abundance. We support each other in living our GENIUS and reaching our goals that we each set for ourselves. I am internally motivated to link my business results to my life goals versus the scarcity of being in a business that will compromise my security if I get off the hamster wheel for personal harmony.

We can disempower our teams with quotas, or we can empower them with personal growth and evolution by empowering them to be true leaders. Consider a salesperson fails to hit goals, and you assess what the salesperson wants to do to get on track and what this course correction to get back on track will mean for the salesperson's life. You get a reason to support them with additional training, and with that training, you prepare the salesperson with what is needed to achieve in the business to get what that salesperson wants in life. Often, your team members do not yet know what they need to get the results they desire when they join you, so you will discuss that more in training.

Scarcity is an unconscious, external gratification, feeding on a need for members to justify their worth, sell more, and finally be good enough. Only they never can be good enough, because a new day, week, month, and target are just a sleep away. Scarcity environments produce burnout, health issues, and an overall lack of genuine support. When you believe the world creates opportunities for you instead of you creating opportunities for yourself—and at the root of this, you also believe that you are not capable or worthy enough to feed, clothe, and provide for yourself—you are also probably willing to cut out others, compete for small advances in your career, and stay stuck in that line hoping someone sees and promotes you. This is a toxic environment.

Abundance is conscious, ever-expanding, with enough opportunity for everyone. Abundance lives to serve and accept. Serve with your unique GENIUS and accept with love, support, and encouragement from the GENIUS of others. There isn't any reason to compare in abundance cultures. We all have different GENIUS and a unique way of approaching the business. This reverence for unique goals and gifts creates a dream team. Everyone in a sales role is armed with the common language of the team in a predictable, tried, tested, and true system. Now, you can honour the unique approach of each sales member, the goals they set, and allow the business to support their unique life goals. You can also help a sales member get to the level of the top sales member much faster. Because you believe in service and believe in results as the metric mirroring your success, support is now part of the greater good to create impact as a team. Everyone helps each other.

Whether you know the air is polluted or not, it is affecting you, and it will affect everyone on your team. The power is to create an environment with a positive effect.

A few fun facts:

- What others around you believe will impact your ability to believe you can change.
- What others achieve in your environment becomes normal. This counts for ultra-performance and sub-par

performance. Normal in one team can be 100 deals per agent, and in another, it could be twenty-five deals. We match the best of our ability in proximity to the average of our environment, not compared to our stand-alone capability to perform.

- Harvard did a thirty-year study that concluded that 95% of success or failure is determined by the people with whom we habitually associate.

Training

One of the biggest indicators of a person's ability to learn and set new habits is that person's personal belief that he or she can change. As Charles Duhigg shares in *The Power of Habit*, "Belief is at the core of modifying many habit loops and plays a critical role in habit change. For habit change to be permanent, people must believe change is possible. Studies show that people must believe in their capacity to change and that things will get better to achieve more permanent habit change."

In a time when boards and licensing bodies seek ways to make training faster, more dramatic, require less of our time and attention, with punchlines to grab our attention, I have a simple question: does it work?

We know the brain requires tension to learn, just like a muscle requires tension to grow at the gym. We can learn, practice, and internalize the equivalent of decades of sales expertise in several weeks, followed by practicing this knowledge until it mixes with our GENIUS and creates the wisdom where we own it. Steven

Covey, a consultant well known for his seven habits of highly effective people theory, established positive judgement as a mixture of technical competence and character. Wisdom is that positive ability to provide valuable judgement to others in a situation that requires your assistance.

There are two areas where we want to consider training. First, when a team member joins our team; and second, ongoing training support.

Onboarding

> *"If we take a man as he is, we make him worse, but if we take man as he should be, we make him capable of becoming what he could be."*
> **—Viktor E. Frankl**

Michelle came into real estate from another industry all together. Well-educated and professional, with strong communication skills and a passion for excellence, Michelle had all the makings of a strong sales agent on paper, but she was lacking the sales skills that would make her a strong candidate for the team leader to hand over costly marketing opportunities. Michelle was part of the first group to go through my new onboarding system. The team leader hired me to train a group of new and experienced sales agents. The agents who "passed" onboarding with me would be given an official welcome into the sales team with access to opportunities, ongoing training, support, and accountability right away.

Michelle went through eight weeks of continuous training. She was taught the beliefs and mindset of a high-performance team. We focused on teaching how a consistently successful agent saw the industry and how this differed from the average agent. We trained on working with buyers and sellers and completing goalsetting to ensure she knew her aim on a weekly basis. She would complete training with the skills to organize, nurture, and convert any opportunity, including the coldest lead sources. This training represents a large puzzle where every piece supports the next and creates the system that leverages the Genius of Michelle as a salesperson with the GENIUS tasks of the other team members.

We do not train all systems together like that anymore. For example, in real estate, we will train on communication patterns, presentations, and language for buyers first. Once that is completed, we go goalsetting to create absolute clarity of what is necessary every day and week. We ramp up, start making some money, and circle back to listing systems later. Michelle did both systems together and was approved for buyer leads just as she started the listing system. Michelle had someone who wanted to think about a buyer representation agreement on her first appointment. When 99.5% of agents would have packed up their things to shake hands and leave, Michelle told me she heard my voice saying people are more afraid of what they do not know than what they do know; take the time to read over the agreement together with the client. At the least, take away the element of the unknown and explain the source of the buyer's agreement; who it was designed to protect; who created it; and when, as salespeople, we are obligated to present this standard agreement to our clients. In the end, the buyer who wanted to think about it hired Michelle that day, as did every other buyer Michelle faced for months. Not because Michelle pushed the client, but because she did not push in the least. Michelle was trained to educate, communicate, and get out of the way once all the factors were discussed to allow a highly intelligent client to choose what was best for them. Michelle was a consultant. With an over 96% conversion rate as a brand-new agent, Michelle was also equivalent to a well-trained sniper. She was worth the investment all day long.

Team leaders love the idea of having a Michelle on their team, but they sell their environment short when they fail to invest in the onboarding and training Michelle needed to get results as one of the sales agents producing predictable results for the team. When you have predictable results, you can more confidently double your investment and, with it, your return. This is the safeguard of scaling. Empower your people with the mindset, confidence, and skillset to excel from the start.

A few weeks later, Michelle completed the Listing System. She came to my home to present at a mock-up listing appointment. The trial run went well and, as with most agents in training, Michelle left with some small areas to improve. We did a second mock-up listing appointment, and Michelle was approved to deliver the standards, communicate guarantees and level of service, and represent the reputation and results of the entire team.

Listing leads are valuable in the real estate industry. Most team leaders hesitate to hand listing opportunities to other team members, as the cost of losing the commission and buyer leads is a decent wager to bet and lose.

A week after her second mock-up listing presentation, Michelle was booked a listing appointment. Upon doing the reminder call, we discovered that the sellers were now interviewing other agents—three others, in fact. We were able to position to sit down with the sellers last, after the seller met with the other agents. However, we learned that the other agents were team leaders attending the appointment themselves, personally, to have an edge competing against Michelle's team.

Michele was a brand new, recently licensed agent when she walked into training with me. She went on her first listing appointment after three established team leaders, each with eight to fifteen years of experience as top producers in our area. They all had strong reputations and came personally to secure the listing contract. Michelle was trained to compete, not with shadowing but with tested skills and strategy. We prepared for these types of situations but never anticipated they would be in place for her first listing appointment. Michelle knew that we did not compare or compete with the competition; instead, we built our own stadiums and invited our clients onto our field to pick which of our services they would like to choose versus if they wanted to choose us.

When the competition tried to convince, push, and sell, we instead educated, consulted, and advocated for our clients. We work with our sellers to empower them to make the best choices for themselves, their families, and their financial outcomes. We trust our clients, and we trust our ability to educate on the options available, and then we let the seller choose.

The seller did choose. They chose Michelle, an agent on her first listing appointment. They hired Michelle to sell their home for over a point more in commission than every other agent quoted the seller. Michelle sat side-by-side with her clients, and she worked with the sellers while the other competing agents debated commission nose-to-nose across the table from the sellers—you could almost say in opposition. And yet Michelle, with less experience, was chosen and paid more. If Michelle was only armed with what to say, it might have been different. If Michelle shadowed to learn what to do, it would take years to garner the average results. Time is money. Results define your business. All results count, too; not just financial.

Michelle knew the psychology behind how people assess information. She knew the psychology of decision making, and she knew the research our sales systems were based on. Michelle had all the factors to create and maintain long-term results.

If we did not create tension at the beginning, Michelle would have been distracted running with leads—distracted because we needed to build her capability to turn those opportunities into results. That capability is most important. *Tension creates focus*, and focus breeds learning.

Entertainment without action is just entertainment. The world may want training turned into a Vegas of learning with consistent social media speed endorphin hits and bright lights, but it does not work. There is no tension, no learning, and very little action.

Your recruits will not want to do this level of training upfront. You will teach them what they need to be a strong agent, and you will protect yourself by investing in team members who are willing to lean into the discomfort of learning and growth to build the life they want.

Your agents will do just under what is required of them. This is not personal to your agents. This is human nature. Most of us will do just under what is required of us to get the job done if we know we can still garner a positive result. Otherwise, we rise to our expectations for ourselves; but even more so, we rise to the expectations of our environment. If we *believe*, it will deliver a greater and more positive result. That requires accountability by you as a team leader to set expectations that lead to your desired results over an agent's desired level of training. Take them where they want to go; and that is not the same as meeting them where they currently are. We rise to our environment or we leave. We do not lean our resources into what is optional in our lives, and team members will not lean their resources into thriving at parts of the business you make optional either.

Manage the system, train, motivate your people, and get out of their way.

> *"What man actually needs is not a tensionless state but rather the striving and struggling for some goal worthy of him. What he needs is not the discharge of tension at any cost, but the call of a potential meaning waiting to be fulfilled by him."*
> **—Viktor E. Frankl**

Ongoing Training Support

Ongoing training is vital to a performance culture. This ongoing training will include a review of the basics taught in your onboarding training and a review of their ability to stay on track with the team's expectations and systems. For example, how many times does an agent on your team need to call a lead before the agent can stop calling? How do you know if it happened? What if they have 300 leads sitting there, called once or never? Do you hold back opportunities until they get caught up? Let the system dictate the expectations to stay on track or to get back on track. This is not personal.

McDonald's requires three pickles on every burger. If you get hired but keep putting two pickles on each burger, someone is going to talk to you; and eventually, you will get a written warning and be let go. You can argue the reasoning of two pickle slices forever. You can cry about your bad day and overwhelming commitments. But at the end of the day, the system says three pickle slices. Three is the recipe for success. One person does not get to break a proven method while delivering to the masses. Those types of changes require testing and a reason to invest resources to investigate the change in the first place. This is your burger, your way, as the customer always experiences it. You can be fast food or gourmet—as long as the experience is delivered consistently.

Weekly and monthly meetings make sense. If you cannot show up consistently for a set meeting, training, or coaching time, then you are also incapable of doubling your business or leading your team. The ability to schedule what will build our future over the instant gratification of the urgent deal with a short-term payoff is vital.

If you cannot make a weekly meeting, neither will your team. There goes your gourmet burger. People could be spitting in the food and serving it on your behalf. You will not know without a training structure.

Mindset

We all have a set point for how we see ourselves and how we see the world. We discussed above that change requires a belief that you are capable of changing and that your changes will build a brighter future for yourself. Another way to look at this is through the lens of growth-or-fixed mindset and leadership-or-victim mentality. The warrior gives his all because that is who the warrior is. The warrior believes his actions define him, and showing up and doing your best to reach your goals defines you. The warrior knows he was built to change, grow, evolve, and ultimately learn and win.

A growth mindset means an individual believes their ability to practice, try, and learn will dictate outcomes; whereas in a fixed mindset, team members only want to do what they feel they are already good at. The fear and discomfort of trying something new and not thriving are overwhelming for someone with fixed mindset. A growth mindset person enjoys learning and challenges. They are great "learners," whereas fixed mindset people take pride in natural talents.

I don't know about you, but I know a lot of people a heck of a lot more talented than me. The only difference between them, me, and you is that they were not willing to show up, try, and risk failure. I am not willing to stand still, and they are not willing to forge forward. I, like you, have the audacity to believe I can succeed. You want to support that mindset in your team members.

The ability to take full responsibility for yourself and your life is the ultimate freedom and the ultimate responsibility. When we build teams with those who are still in line waiting for someone to see them, pick them, and promote them, we build with people who believe life is done onto them. They succeed or they fail, and none of it has anything to do with them. These people are dangerous. They will erode the team and their ability to succeed slowly, and if they are very committed to their victimhood, they may make some progress. Therefore, team values and culture need to be conscious, strong, and eventually, self-governing. You want to bring these conversations into your team so you can support personal leadership and 100% responsibility as vital to a performance culture.

I once had a team member who would send in work with errors—missing key dates and vital parts of the project. We were set up to fail the minute the project hit our ideal clients. If I would provide feedback, the team member felt he could never win and "why even try", as I would only change his work. Despite agreeing on the final project and serving our clientele as a priority, this behaviour continued. The mistakes grew, and I was in a double bind. If I said something, I was communicating that the work was not good enough; and if I did not say anything, I was compromising results and failing to support our team. Adding to those complications, when I did not say something, I was also told that I was not taking responsibility for the team as the leader. Talk about lose-lose. There was no personal leadership here. Once the unconscious became conscious, I started to see the pattern. We discussed the issue, and I attempted to set boundaries to protect the team and encourage the team member. This became a slippery slope, and slide we did—relatively fast.

If you are a leader who is focusing on self-leadership, you may assume others will act and lead themselves as you do. This is not a reality. Everyone is different and sees the world with their own unique lens. People with a victim mindset view the world as a victim. They are always being wronged and can never be good enough, so why should they try? They will use these beliefs to justify their actions and claim they are wronged when you, again, seek a direct conversation. The victim mindset is a belief about how you see the world. To change these deep beliefs requires resources, a willingness to explore the root of the belief, and an immense amount of courage to face a different way of seeing the world. It takes courage to say, "Wait, I am creating this." Many of us were there. To open the source of a victim mindset can be painful and confusing. Vulnerability without resources is cruel punishment.

You cannot make anyone want to change their mindset. Performance comes from leading one's self and owning 100% of the results in your environment. That goes for sales members and for you as a leader. You are 100% responsible for everything that happens in your environment. If you, as the leader, cannot make the choices and the changes to protect your clients and the business, then who can?

When hiring or recruiting, listen for indicators of abundance, growth, and leadership mindsets. Training yourself to watch for the whispers of someone attracted to your environment on a personal journey to evolve, and change may come also. The best teams create leaders. The environment is more powerful in the final performance of a sales member than their natural talent; however, the best environment can only win with a mind open to its influence. You can start small, but the victim mindset is independent in its gaze, whereas the leadership mindset is impact-minded in its perspective.

Victims have reasons for lacking results. Leaders have results created by their reasons.

Accountability (Capability)

Accountability includes a willingness to view your capabilities, celebrate your strengths, and leverage the GENIUS of others to improve your own skillset in your role. With a team, you are doing a fraction of a full sales role per salesperson. Even sales members do a highly modified version of the typical sales role. This means that you need to ensure you have results. You are taking on lower cost activities and/or tasks that require more energy and time for salespeople to complete and moving those to others. You are paying for others to do those tasks that are undesirable to a sales agent. High-performing salespeople want to live in the fast lane doing what they do best. The more you take the tasks a salesperson sees as tedious and time-consuming off the salesperson's plate, the more deals the salesperson will do and the happier the salesperson will be. Everyone has better results, including the client who gets the most valuable aspects of the sales agent to support them. This all means you need to provide a world-class experience for clients so you can get results and have the income to pay others to live in their GENIUS, which will free you to live in yours.

What does this have to do with accountability? Everything!

Tracking ensures you can make changes faster, predict future production sooner, and keep your finger on the pulse of the business. You need to know how you're performing from opportunity to client, client to deal, and past client to valued member of your community. Members of your community are happy to help and recommend you and your team; they trust you, and trust you will take care of their family and friends. As a solo agent, you are risking your own time and money when you operate below the capability available for a salesperson in the industry. Often, as an individual sales agent, you may not even be conscious of the losses operating below capability is costing you, because what do you have to compare to?

On a team, you are investing in marketing, lead generation, support people, and your time to train and nurture sales talent. There is quite a risk in not knowing the source of business for each transaction. This can lead to overinvesting in marketing or lead generation without realizing that it is bringing you little to no return. A separate and extremely important consideration is the risk of giving opportunities to a sales agent who is not converting. The loss in both areas are exponential. Either you lose potential business putting your lead generation dollars in the wrong place, or you lose potential business by investing leads you have with agents consistently delivering a lower rate of return for themselves and the business. Think about opportunity lost multiplied by your average potential commission earned. For most teams, these types of losses are worth hundreds of thousands of dollars per year.

Capability comes first, then opportunity. Accountability comes in the form of metrics that show capability at work with tracked results. Accountability is also a part of a personal leadership mindset to take responsibility for your results, celebrate your wins, course-correct when needed, and see the results that empower everyone with the ability to seek the resources they need to do what they want.

GENIUS

Living in your Genius is where the money, energy, and time live. Living in your Genius allows you to bring your gifts to the world while nurturing your gifts in your everyday work. The GENIUS model is ever-evolving to eventually carve down to a business for yourself and your team, where you do the highest portions of your work in an area that energizes you, fulfills you, and brings the best of your work to the world. You have the most prosperity in your area of Genius because it is worth the most to your teams and clients.

Allow your team members the privilege of moving more and more into their Genius as they evolve with their capabilities and results. Create a system to transparently identify when additional leverage is available to allow for greater production at a higher caliber and in less time.

Mastery Is Forgetful

By its very nature, mastery is a forgetful force. The human brain never remembers something the same way twice. As you learn, experience, grow, and—hopefully—evolve, you are investing in an ever-expanding set of eyes. The eyes you have now are the only ones that will ever see what you are currently thinking about, watching, saying, learning, or even remembering. The eyes I once used to learn a communication technique are now changed. Overall, this is a good thing, as it means we are self-renewing, learning more, and increasing our ability to bring value to the world. This is how I believe you recharge yourself toward worthwhile work, avoid burnout, and live in an intrinsic inspiration model. However, where predictable systems are involved, understanding of the human mind presents a unique challenge.

Because we never remember something the same way twice, we need to reset even in mastery. Ongoing training is what keeps us at the level we are. The public will train a team member more efficiently than our systems due to negative reinforcement alone. Every time a client chooses another agent, a lead hangs up on us, or we discover a client is not happy—those experiences etch beliefs in the mind of the sales agent. Even if that same approach was successful 98 out of 100 times, it will now start to adjust based on the two clients who gave negative feedback directly or by way of choosing the competition. On the inverse, you can have a one-off success that will cause a sales agent to adjust away from consistent, proven methods. One-on-one disappointments or wins are a strong reinforcement for how to do business, but data and predictable results build a business, and often, the two tell a very different story. Therefore, to reset with training means we create confidence, preparing for all likely scenarios upfront.

Mastery is nuanced. To understand nuance, you must live among it, bathe in it, and breathe it. Mastery becomes the essence of us. We practice mastery without thinking. Mastery turns what you consciously practiced and learned with a presentation and script and reinforces new neural pathways every time you practice. Or, it alters that same slide or script until you eventually create an unconscious pathway in your brain where very little to no conscious processing is required. This is when you successfully turn something that you consciously knew you did not know into something you know and, finally, into something you know unconsciously. This is where you can learn a dance while focusing 100% on your partner, the crowd, and the room. The dance no longer requires any mental bandwidth or conscious focus. Your body remembers the steps in line with the rhythm of the song. You internalized the movements and words of the song into a dance fully in flow. Similar to a presentation where you have full focus on a client while your body knows to have your finger click next on the laptop to move the slides without needing to look at the screen or visually assess which slide is next.

Ruthless Leadership Aligned around the Ultimate Value

"No one can become fully aware of the very essence of another human being unless he loves him."
—Viktor E. Frankl

Whenever we are in search of advice, leadership, and next steps, we need to have clear guiding principles established. Hopefully, you still have time to establish these principles in advance. If not, what better time to start than now?

I am a big fan of working out terms of engagement for difficult situations and fierce conversations. I also advocate for creating an exit strategy for anything while everyone is happy and on their best behaviour. This includes team agreements, guiding principles, and leadership guidelines.

You need a few North Stars for when the going gets tough. For most top producers turned Team Leaders, the people management is often the most difficult aspect. When you are growing, you need to manage and leverage to create a performance environment for everyone. If you want a big team, there may come a time when people management moves into a "Neutral," "Includes Others," "Unconscious Incompetence," or "Stop" task on your GENIUS Model.

This does not mean you will stop motivating and leading the team. It means that you move some of the management portions of leadership to another team member who thrives in that area. Most high drivers are self-starters and struggle with others who do not self-start to their level.

True North Guiding Principles

The ultimate of all values and intentions is love. Love is, at times, outspoken in its service to others. Love has no issue with acting in service of others. Love does not care to be your best friend. Love looks to build others up or clean others off to see their true self. Love looks for GENIUS and is a warrior in protecting our highest of intentions to serve.

What could be a better value to guide a business, family, community, country, and world? Love is universal.

We work off of the principle that we love our clients. I say this openly on stages and on coaching calls. This is not an easy principle for some to equate with business at times. Perhaps we speak so much about love in families and romantic relationships that it is easy to forget love applies to everything we do well and is missing in all we do that breaks us down.

What is to come?

The following chapter is devoted to synergy. I promise you one thing. Once you feel what it is like to have a team in synergy, nothing else will feel as fulfilling, capable, or rewarding. We are forever course-correcting toward the path, and toward a future outcome, and to travel there in synergy is to travel in timeless fashion sense and style.

Maybe because I will forever have a weak spot for the elusive green light, for the dreamers who stretch out toward the future, extending their arms and bodies beyond safety with little preventing them from falling, with the naive belief that someday, if they just stretch far enough, they will touch the future they crave in their hands. Forever waiting for life to allow them to pursue and touch an outcome in unison. When the love of pursuing something more important than ourselves is the goal, path, journey, and outcome all in one.

A top-producing, top 1% team achieves the outcome which matches their mindset, environment, training, accountability, and GENIUS. The result mirrors them. The only thing we are then chasing is the future version of ourselves.

To feel the flow of a high-performance team, doing what they do best, working in their level of GENIUS, aligned toward a common outcome, carving their path by the values they believe in, and nurturing together is the ultimate experience. It is worth course-correcting back to, and it is worth building into existence. This type of movement attracts like-minded people and creates an unstoppable vortex for as long as it stays intact.

Chapter 11
BUILT TO WIN: TEAM SYNERGY

So many are stuck in a vicious cycle. The dog keeps chasing its tail, and as soon as it thinks it is close enough to bite the thing, it misses again. Everyone loves an underdog. They have so much heart, but there are some places that heart needs a little soul and strategy to help it along. That underdog is not done; the dog will never give up chasing its tail, and in some ways, as an underdog, neither will you. That dog will get up and chase the unreachable, forever left exhausted but undeterred. In the sales world, this looks a little more like burnout, sadness, and despair.

The underdog will get up again, and eventually, so will you. The difference between the stunningly successful and the overworked underachiever is an awareness of options. When we see the choices, the paths appear. Until you invest in learning your options, you stay stuck. The stunningly successful and the overworked underachiever choose different options, but only one of the two knew they had multiple options to start with.

As Robert Frost said, "Two roads diverged in a wood, and I took the one less traveled by, and that has made all the difference." You have two choices in your plight to build your life back: To either chase your tail endlessly in a work harder, self-employed, gross earnings world of the overworked underachiever; or break free, take an educated risk, and build your exit strategy with a firm resolution to live in ultimate freedom, carving your own way of living and making your own choices your way. This is the life of the stunningly successful.

Your Genius is meant to thrive. While the sun still shines behind the clouds, above the thunder, and even behind the lightening, during a tropical storm or hurricane, the sun still works hard doing its job hidden above and behind; but no one talks about the sunshine when they can't see it or feel it.

We market to get busy; when we get too busy to serve our clients, we end up with no time to elevate our services and no extra time for ourselves. You keep reaching for the dollars but fail to build what will bring you the consistent client flow you need. You keep chasing your tail. One day, you will have enough time to build a business that can support more clients, service them with excellence, and attract new clients all at once.

The underdog keeps trying, eating into his personal time, while filling the funnel with sales prospects and bills to pay. He needs to get busy now. But the stunningly successful business owner knows better. She saw the underachiever sell out his dreams trying to be all things to all people, trapped forever in various phases of scarcity, forever looping back into the same place, always behind, always lacking.

Within two months of building my latest company, I was over my desired max capacity for one-on-one coaching clients and teams. I was doing all the client memberships, assessments, personality profiles, setting up payments, accounting, marketing, training at various offices, with a dream to serve. If I called it a win and celebrated success at that point, I would still be there at that same level of business. I was capped; I had no more time, energy, or resources without getting help. I capped several times since that point, and I will keep capping out, but never at the same place—and that is the key. You know you are growing when you relieve time in one area of your business—like administration, for example—and all that time is filled with opportunities within a few weeks. We only see the opportunity we have room for.

As a coach, when I am onstage, I am not face-to-face with clients; and when I am face-to-face serving clients, I am not onstage. In both cases, I am also unable to attend to any other areas of the business. Speaking, strategy, and coaching all fall within my Genius. Those are the areas where I provide the most value to the world and where I bring unique experience and expertise. Even with these areas falling in my Genius, I still began to cap my time. The more I speak, share, and train, the less time I must nurture the very people investing in our solutions to create results for our clients. The results of our clients represent the income that supports my team and company.

It means you are constantly swaying between the extremes of having clients and finding clients, to the loss of all the important stuff in between which can give you consistent clients and free your time up. In my business, this also leaves the world wondering where all the clients keep going. In a solo-faced coaching business, you are in the same feast-or-famine as anyone in the sales industry.

In the sales world, this focus on new or existing business only and one at a time impacts your repeat and referral business, as you have less time to consistently nurture relationships that do not represent business now. This approach trains your brain to be transactional and justifies the means with the end. You must pay your bills and survive, right? This transactional nature of sales keeps you locked into the revolving pattern even more, and with active clients, you have an abundance of current opportunity but a scarcity of time and security. Without active clients, you have an abundance of time but a scarcity of security and opportunity. You need to leverage out some of the vital functions that build the flow of business and opportunities to create consistent opportunities, time, and security flowing together all at once.

By building a team, I can help new people and do what I love, sharing it with an audience. I can oversee client resource updates on our members' vault to make sure our clients can implement them right away. I can create new masterminds and online coaching to bring our community together to support each other. And I can train coaches to guide, support, and coach our clients along the way. I could build an entire team to support myself being face-to-face with clients and on stage 90% of the time, but I would still cap out and become stuck between sharing our message, extending our brand, and serving our valued clients. This approach limits my potential business growth. It fails to allow others an opportunity to thrive on the platform I built. It ties my hands in mentorship and service to foster other valuable coaches that our industry needs more than ever. And eventually, it will lead to me have the biggest of disappointments when my potential to share my GENIUS with the world is compromised. I will disappoint my clients if I am without enough time to balance the most important facets of my life. I am responsible for honouring the opportunities presented in front of me and nurturing the paths that appear. When we know better, we do better. You lead your ship, and now you can lead your business for success. This is a critical shift.

Salespeople do not make a team; people make a team. Licensed, unlicensed, clients, family, friends, and everyone else who supports us—they all play a part in a successful team.

Those late nights when someone is at home holding down the fort, when your family steps in to help you get things done for a family dinner, or you cancel on the dinner last minute—those moments all took a team. The more organized your business is, the less of a load everyone in it must carry. This includes you; but it also means reducing the stress and sacrifices of your loved ones.

For those solo parents, you have children co-creating this business with you. Those children are part of your team. I suggest you start recruiting them. Children can want to support you or make your life a living hell. Give them the ability to prosper with you by setting family goals and working together. When I am stuck and need to push through hard decisions and difficult situations, there are many times I asked myself, "What would you want your daughter to do? What would you want your son to choose?" And if I really want to give myself a kick in the butt, I ask, "What would your sister say?"

In the end, we want to build the world we wish for our loved ones. Building a team based in love makes everyone involved your loved ones. Would you do it for your clients? What about your children? Your spouse? Your friends? Your parents? Your family?

When is it time to make the changes that you need for yourself?

You can build a one-face show with a team behind the scenes making as much happen as possible without you, but you are capped, and the business is worthless—literally, because the business is still essentially all you. You are building an unfair personal advantage with a false sense of abundance. All the leads that the team creates come to you on this one-face team, which would not be the case with other sales agents. You are overpaid for your portion of the sales as you pocket everything after expenses. This skews what a sales role is actually worth in your mind, creating a belief that others will not work for less than you do, but you are likely not even working for what you think you are worth. You are more than likely combining those views on the stadium from the owner's box and leader's bench and attributing all the money to you and the sales players on the field. That gross income mindset caps you every time. There is no leverage, profit, or scalable expansion when you count all income as sales income.

When you are sick or on holiday, you will lose money on potential business and overpay for outside licensed help. You are limiting both of the two-core, income-producing roles in the business by being the only sales agent: sales and lead generation. The likelihood that you can follow up and nurture all business opportunities created by a growing team yourself are slim to none. Everything is flowing to you, and that is an inherent weakness and risk to the business. What if you have the flu horribly one year, want more family time, have a family emergency, or develop a chronic or terminal illness? What if a loved one passes away? You are the business, and the entire team is there only to support you, not an overall business capable of thriving. A whole is always greater than any one of its individual parts. This is not the case for your business. All of this combined creates a false sense of abundance.

Energy is energy, and it will go in the path of least resistance, continuing the momentum it began with, and that momentum should be leverage. You have a taste of the power of leverage or at least the vision of it now. You can train your brain to recognize and encourage GENIUS in yourself and others. In looking for GENIUS, nurturing it, training it into capability, and partnering with it, you get to build a business that gives you the harmony in your life which you seek, which led you to buy this book.

GENIUS lives and thrives in synergy with other evolving minds and conscious souls all working together toward a common purpose. Your business makes a difference. It has the capability to serve the world far beyond the needs of one single self. You may find your business will build a platform for others to find the harmony they seek in their lives along with you. You may find that others will become trained experts faster working with you. You may find that this impacts the way you see your industry and shows you another path in contributing to the elevation of your profession overall.

We all have an ego, and we all want security by nature, even if we mask that security in the face of a solo sales role leading the show. It is still playing smaller than a strong business is built to play. You are creating a business that is bigger than you, and in stepping into that future, you will attract, support, and thrive with others who put impact above profit; who will passionately meet and exceed your brand standards and service levels; and who will partner, nurture, support, and celebrate GENIUS with you.

The ability to maintain the sales level you thrive at now will be more and more challenged as an individual agent. I believe you are already being challenged on your own through using traditional approaches to build your sales business that are now falling short and can no longer deliver the results they once did—also in competing with teams of specialists when you are trying to be all of the hats sales now require of you. I also see most individual agents lost in confusion as to the actual value and worth of their role in the industry today, whether due to technology changes, access to information, or the advancement of the sales process. This confusion impacts your ability to compete for business. It steals your competitive edge. This will all mean less money, increased scarcity, and less time away from your business.

Fear always paralyzes some and motivates others. Fear is for people who have two paths and do not know which to choose. The fearful are better resourced than the overworked underachievers who see one path and proceed falsely optimistic down that path. They are hopeful that they are doing the best they can on the only route there is: hard work. A team provides shelter and a competitive advantage in a changing industry. A team is an investment in elevating your service and resources to potential and current clients. A team extends the longevity of your business.

I have faith in the abundance of an ever-evolving world. I have faith in people who can hold contrasting truths, perspectives, and beliefs, all with a loving understanding of how another could choose that very set of perspectives, even if I would not choose them myself. There is validity in all angles. This is the GENIUS team. The GENUIS team knows that we all have blind spots and strengths, and it knows that they allow us to combine perspectives and turn a flat picture into a multi-dimensional view. Team mentality is changing the world. The driver is not always the best to decide.

Just this week, I heard of an initiative of a high driver team leader. The team sales member acknowledged that the team leader put a plan in place that was not sustainable with the budget. The program just did not work. The frustrated sales agent, having built growth around the plan, left the team. What the sales agent did not know was that the team manager asked me to review the plan years ago. I forecasted the growth of the program over time, and it clearly would not work. We already knew the eventual end of the program, and the team leader, eager to motivate the team, had good intentions, albeit short-sighted. The leader took a one-dimensional solution from one perspective only—his—and it cost the team.

The future is built on leveraging strengths to go faster, further, and better informed, together.

> *Do I contradict myself? Very well, then I contradict myself, I am large, I contain multitudes.*
> —**Walt Whitman**

Chapter 12

NOW OR NEVER, YOUR PROBLEM IS THE SOLUTION

S ome of the changes we reviewed together will seem scary. Most people will resist anything that seems scary or uncomfortable at first. Some people resist for longer than others, and some resist stubbornly forever.

The committed will resist first, then embrace change second.

Every great idea that will change your business will feel scary at first. The magic combination of great goals is fear and excitement. Not fear alone or excitement alone. You need both.

Any great idea that doesn't scare you may not be that worthwhile. Remember, you are becoming a leader who, in the future, will not be scared by these ideas; and if you were already that person and leader, then why would you be scared?

Believe in the GENIUS of Change

In the summer of 2016, my world started to spin—literally. I came home from the cottage with my son and was rushing around the house in our usual system—the kids unpacking the car while I put all the food away, took the dirty clothes upstairs, started laundry ASAP, and brought all bags to the right rooms and unpacked. I learned that with a workweek about to start the following day, anything else besides immediate action is impossible to manage cottage weekends. My children would only take their bags into their rooms, leave them as is, add to them for packing a week later—and I learned to live with that. Dirty clothes into one bag before we left the cottage resolved the biggest issues, and we had the groove down to the "T" for the past few years.

I remember one odd weekend where my daughter was with her father, and Ethan, my son, was with me. I dropped him off to his dad for a family dinner and walked back up to my spare room where the next load of laundry was waiting for me. As I turned to put a shirt into the wardrobe, the world started to shake. I grabbed the bed to try and stabilize myself, as I was sure we were having an earthquake. It took some time to identify my world was shaking and not the actual house. I was staring out, looking for a calm and stable view, but none could be had because the shaking was coming from me.

If you never had an experience like this, I will full on admit that it was terrifying. I was alone in the house, so I decided to have a "suck it up buttercup" pep talk moment over going to the hospital.

I decided to lie down and felt a bit better. After attempting laundry one more time, I realized I would have to go to bed for the night. I am a pretty active person, and the weekend was no different—stand up paddleboard trips, swimming, and walking. At home, I go to hot power yoga and/or run five to six times a week. I have a regiment to build and maintain the energy I need to do the things I want, which all led to this earthquake experience seeming quite off.

I remember opening my eyes the next morning to a stable view of my ceiling. I was instantly hopeful—maybe it was just some slight case of heatstroke or sunstroke. When my feet hit the ground—boom, earthquake all over again. I was not spinning but completely disoriented. Over the next two weeks, my legs and arms went almost numb. I had pins and needles so strong it became hard to walk. I could drive but would become exhausted quickly. Luckily, the kids and I had holidays planned the following week. I was still not well but wanted to go, and we set out for camping at Bon Echo Provincial Park in Ontario, Canada. The park was just under two hours from our cottage. It's a special place I love to visit.

Bon Echo is considered sacred ground by the natives, and, to this day, people travel there for spirit quests. I was sure I was in the right place to find clarity and realign myself. The kids wanted to pack up and go—"Why are we camping when we have a cottage? "

A small bonus was the restricted cell signal. This was exactly where I needed to be: quiet, calm, with nature, healing, and at peace.

Back at home, my business was busier than ever. We were expanding with more clients, coaches, and staff. I was still overseeing everything, but I did not come to terms with the fact that I was physically exhausted carrying a business on my own. I would quickly watch the business unravel to see I was carrying the plates of almost everyone on the team. The people who should have been helping and supporting our growth had 101 excuses for why I should carry their plates and be grateful for the chance to do so.

Leaving my past business shook me up, and I was operating in a false sense of abundance I brought the team as well as over-inflating the security or value they brought me. All of this combined in creating some small ripples of scarcity. In slight moments of scarcity, I could still reach for the stars, but I could not enforce the boundaries of a performance culture. I did not want to risk the business or compromise our clients with a disruption. When we ignore the knocks of the world at our door, fortunately, it knocks louder to get our attention.

The problem with caring about your business and clients too much is that you will pick up the plates. Those plates most importantly represent promises to people who put their faith in you, who took a chance on you first. Those people are your clients. The plates also represent duties, tasks, values, and commitments of your team members that are hired to help the business provide to clients. They are hired to help keep promises that the team needs to believe in together. Some leaders attempt to carry these plates as a badge of honour; others carry the plates to protect their clients; and others carry the plates with a lack of training, resulting in a lack of trust for the team members' capabilities in completing work to your standards as a leader. Regardless of why you are picking up other people's plates and carrying them on your own, the reality is that you will fail. You cannot make people believe what you do, deliver to your standards, or even play fair. You may have the business you do because you are a giver, and—like me—you love your clients, you love your team, and you want to serve a greater purpose to the best of your ability.

The problem is that you will get busy; you will need to rely on your team, and you cannot carry your team and yourself. You cannot live in your GENIUS behind the clouds of a dysfunctional team. The team members need to be empowered to live in their GENIUS with full autonomy to thrive and excel in their roles. It is not your responsibility to care enough for everyone. It is your responsibility to care enough to hire the right people; arm them with the training and culture to excel; and insist that the team operates to serve the business and clients within the highest intentions of honesty, love, and purpose. If you have people on your team who cannot or will not take responsibility for the results they bring to the team, for living to the capability of their GENIUS, and the vision of the team, then it is your responsibility to stop and change anything that will harm the business's ability to offer ever-increasing services and results to your clients.

No one team member is worth capping the capability and results of the business because that capability, in full, is defined as your client experience and results.

You will be tired. You will get tired.

You will get busy. You will get busier.

You will think this is all easy as you read this book.

GENIUS mastered looks simple only from the outside.

You will think you can recreate the wheel and win.

You will think your problems are unique to your market and industry.

You will think you need custom solutions for your unique problems.

You will think you can hire someone to solve this for you.

You will think you can figure it out as you go.

You may burn out.

You may get sick.

You may end a relationship.

You may have team members burn you and leave you without notice.

It is a lonely and hard road building a business on your own.

You may want someone in your corner.

You may want some support.

You may feel like it is you against the world.

You may feel judged, alone, and confused.

You may feel like quitting.

You may want to decide that I am full of it. It is an easy out.

You may think that giving up on getting some help will take stress off your plate. It won't.

Attending events and seeing others who achieved what you want *will* propel you and your team to build.

It could take you ten years to perfect a system, or you can model and implement one in two years or less. I know this because I did not just build one team. I worked with thousands of agents to build their businesses and hundreds more to build top 1% producers and seven-figure earners with more free time and enhanced quality of life. I helped teams multiply their business by 1000%, also known as 10X growth. We have worked with Top Producers to multiply their business by 2000%, or 20X Growth in their business. You are facing the same problems and same potential solutions that they were. The question is how long and at what cost will you continue to stay where you are? Are you willing to see and take the second path to be stunningly successful? Do you have the personal resources to thrive on your own, or do you need some help?

It turns out what was now being labelled vertigo, with no appropriate testing what-so-ever, got worse. Standing in a grocery store in Cloyne, Ontario, with massive sensory overwhelm, my son said, "Mom, let's go home. You look like you are dying."

He was right. I mean, I do not know what I will look like when I die—hopefully old, happy, and ready to fall asleep at 184 years old. This was not my vision. I was pale, overwhelmed physically, emotionally, and mentally tired in my soul. I was fighting for a team dream all on my own, and as I moved back into an abundance and leadership mentality in the coming weeks, I also owned up to it all being my responsibility. Changes should have been made long ago. There was no excuse for the behaviour for leadership on my team, and the worst part? What type of a leader was I for allowing it and covering up the facts to give myself fake comfort, denying the truth, turning away from the path so beautifully gifted for me to see, and turning away from the choices I should not make by doing the extra work myself? This was long a "me" problem. You get what you tolerate. I would never allow a client to tolerate what I did without a fight. I would advocate for them to the point where they may fire me, but I would not allow that client to do what I did—never.

The wrong people working the right systems is worse than no team and no systems at all. I was a team builder facing sabotage by the very people who should have been supporting the team, and despite me doing their workloads, they were recruiting others to help them in a "coup" against the very company they were obligated to protect.

The vertigo was the business, and the business was vertigo. I was trying to hold it all on my own. I remember one night working on a proposal for myself and another team member to speak at a series of events being held by a regional real estate board. I was working days, nights, and weekends for almost two years. I made the commitment to go all-in for two years when I opened this business. Kids, coaching, and exercise—yes, let's do this. Well, time was ticking, and the vertigo was right on time to remind me that time was up, and it was here to deliver my wake-up call.

As we discussed the proposal, I heard "dinner" called out from the house of the other phone line. The team member excused themselves from the call, and I continued to work on the proposal. With two kids of my own to feed, I felt like something was broken here. A few hours later, I would receive my team member's portion of the proposal only 20% complete and due that night. I spent another two hours completing the full speaker proposal package. Our proposals had to be sent together, and as I crawled into bed late that night, I felt it coming. Another "SCREW THIS" moment. The combination of vertigo, quick business growth, life, business demands, and a growing concern for the quality of content provided and the protection being delivered to our clients had all combined and was now coming to a head. It was all too much, and yet, just enough to start to make some decisions. I would not live like this anymore, and the business would support our clients to the standard I provided for years. Our clients hired our reputation, so it was up to me to ensure that was restored and delivered.

As with any "SCREW THIS" moment, the tip of the iceberg prompted it. The full iceberg that would come to be displayed was wide and deep. The world gave me the perfect storm to say enough, to take the reins back, to stop feeding the dragon once again, and to build the business and life I was capable of building. I would walk onto the stage at the largest team-specific summit in real estate two days after informing my team that key team members had been let go. It was a pivotal moment in choosing the business because the business was chosen by our coaches and clients. The world is a mirror, and it will mirror your process with results or a noticeable lack of results. Our job is to build with an ever-continuing course correction toward what is honest, true, and right. We forever course-correct toward delivering the results we promise to the public. To advertise something, you cannot provide energy that is not aligned with business expansion. We promote to the public with the potential gains we can provide; we provide the journey to those results and an ongoing value exchange that is driven by purpose and reward with compensation or gross earnings. If what you are doing does not provide what is advertised, you can stop advertising it or insist on restoring the systems and tools that brought you the results you built your business on in the first place.

I rarely work with a team leader who does not have to level up their standards in the name of client service and face the potential of losing team members or clientele. But here is the thing: I faced losing half of our client base when I let those team members go; but on the other hand, I faced losing our entire business, my capability to live my purpose, and our capability as a team to deliver what was possible if I did not let them go. We did lose half the clients, but we gained double of that loss back in the same year. I found out later from our coaches that those same members were informing coaches to tell prospective clients to wait to sign up for coaching as we approached an annual event held by our company. This was a six-figure event and our top way of connecting with new sales agents and teams needing our help. They would build a new company with my content and sign the clients who attended the event to this new company after our company event was over. Why not use our marketing and event budget to fund this new company? I only found all of this out later because the coaches did not do this and could not because the changes were made just in time. I failed to act when I could have, but the world gave me another chance to act, and I took it.

The values of our leaders are contagious, just like the values we bring to the business ourselves. We attract who we are.

In the end, everyone has a place and a purpose. Actions that are not aligned in your business are a red flag begging your attention to serve with love. Lack of alignment is an indicator of an ill fit.

All people have a gift to provide this world, but not in your business, on your dime, or on your time if they cannot believe in your purpose and serve the business to its standards.

Vertigo, along with all the expansion and management issues, was my red flag. The obstacles will beg you to see them as a chance to level up. Luckily, I coached the answers for years, and when everything hit the fan, I heard the voice of systems, grounded down to core principles, and looked up to see the vision and purpose of our business. I heard decades of team development and millions worth of trial and error. I knew what worked. I had a voice whispering to me, and I want you to have that voice in your ear too.

All these years of clients sharing times when they faced difficulty and heard my voice carving the way. I was happy they persevered and prevailed. I never knew I would hear that same coaching voice one day. We all face difficulty, we all stumble, and we all have the ability to course-correct when the world gifts us with awareness delivered in difficulty. I was so busy trying to keep everything afloat, I failed to see that I was already under water. Thank goodness the world got my attention. The world calls out and begs for the attention of thousands of leaders like you and me. Those calls give us the moment of calm we need to set a new plan in that brief chance we have, to stand strong in the eye in the storm, where we can build what is possible, take the reins, and build a business that has our back. That moment is your chance to buy your own glass slippers and kiss the frog that is in all things owning your gifts, giving yourself permission, promotion, and privilege to do what it takes and be what it takes to have your cake and eat it too. Not just for your team members, but for your family, community, the world, and yourself.

It is not by accident that every time a team member left, someone more in line with my team's energy, focus, and conviction arrived. We get what we tolerate, and "SCREW THIS", I was just not willing to live that way anymore. The right people show up when we are ready because our energy and frequency calls to a new level. We cannot push others to be what we want. We can expect what others are capable of in their GENIUS and support their growth with an environment that expects and demands our best; and if any one of your team members won't give their best, the environment chooses the dream over them, as it should. The business is the guiding light. I am my clients, and my clients are me. We are building a business with our hearts. We are exploring the limits of what is possible, and most of all, we are willing to take a beating trying to build a great life, but often we are doing it for everyone else. I want to help you to build with ease. I want to help you build something that serves everyone else and you. We make the right choices inside, get the resources we need, and we move forward. We can get stuck in the everyday to-dos or we can carve the next edition of ourselves, our business, and our lives. We carve out what is possible in ourselves to bring those changes to our world.

Remember, 100 pennies a day. Do not give away your pennies for penny returns; save some of them every day for the future you want. Guard that time and energy—that ability to decide what is important today—and tomorrow is your gold. Believe you can make your business better with the right help.

Chapter 13
FORGET A TOP 1% BUSINESS, I WANT A TOP 1% LIFE

"Love is the ultimate and highest goal"
—Viktor E. Frankl

For a long time, they would not let me on their stages. So, I built my own. Some of us are not here to fit into this world. We are here to build our own worlds, contributing to a greater shift in the world. We are here to live through and into the changes we seek.

No one is rescuing you, me, or anyone else from the demands of business. There is no magical recruitment fairy who shows up and says you are perfect to lead this existing team with everything you need, with more time off, an already organized business, help you can rely on, and a raise!

The line for the magical recruitment fairy who sees your potential, your GENIUS, and has the perfect role to give you the life you want is as long as this earth is round. There is no end to that line, and no one is ever chosen, but people keep showing up, waiting, hoping, and wishing.

I wrote this book because I see people get stuck waiting for life to change for them. I see this each and every day. My team and I do strategy calls with those looking to build their business. We offer free business assessments on our website and reports on the shifts in the industry to nurture the perspective that gives you a new path and builds the business to give you the life you want.

We run the largest team-specific summit in the real estate industry, called Ultimate Team Summit, to bring people together who want to build and grow faster. They support each other, refer to each other, and show each other what is possible.

With all of this, we still get the calls every year. I remember speaking with a team leader who was distraught about his business taking all his time. He did nothing to change it. Every year, he would call and chat about the business he wanted. One year, he noticed one of our clients had another "explosive growth year," and he felt this client was set to do the same thing again.

The client he was referring to started coaching around the same time that this gentleman started calling us. Our client had a business three times the earnings and three times the team size and was enjoying a strong harmony of work and personal time with his family.

After asking what this client was doing, our team wished him well, and he went on to have the same conversations, same number of transactions, and same earnings year after year. Team building becomes exponential in growth after two years with our tools. Despite all of the clients who double their business in year one with us, this is actually not where the most profound growth happens. At the two to five-year phase, we see a massive divide. Those focusing on one-face style sales business or average team building now have a massive gap in earning and sales performance compared to those thriving with the Ultimate Expansion Strategy. The Ultimate Expansion Strategy builds a foundation for a real business worthy of scale. Filling the holes in the bucket for first and second-year growth is just the beginning.

At the end of the day, you are the fuel that will power any strategy, system, tool, sales training, or communication strategy. You will decide how well any tool works in your business based on the confidence, implementation, and energy with which you engage those systems and tools. You are your business, you are the vision of growth for your business, and you are your own business limitations also.

My wish for you is to be so aligned, confident, and resolved at what you need in this life that you see your worth and build the business you are capable of to serve yourself, your future team, your clients, your family, your community, and the world. I hope you see your capabilities, take back the reigns, build a business that has your back, and kick some serious butt. Why? Because sales is a ruthless master.

We got into this business to protect and provide for our families, but not at the expense of rarely seeing them or lacking presence when we are home. We got into this business to give ourselves the freedom to choose how we wanted to live and support our families. We discovered we could support many families and our community. We discovered people relied on our promises in times of difficulty and fear. We discovered that sales are not sales at all, but rather showing care, concern, and protection while delivering the results of our promises. That, to me, is a statement of love.

The best in sales love what they do and love the people they protect. The best in sales fail to love themselves when they build businesses that provide for everyone else, leaving them tied to selling, unable to step back, obligated to continue to lead, and with little worth in selling their business.

I wrote this book as a wake-up call to protect yourself. I am here to fight for the team leader. When the team leader builds better business models, the industry benefits with increased services, training, standards, and professionalism. Team leaders can build their business with passion while rebelling against an industry that pressures them to build using advice in spite of themselves. You can have more time with your family and deliver a better client experience. You can hire others who believe in your vision, and that vision becomes part of their own. You can hire people who will take responsibility for the promises your business makes. You can get organized and you can thrive together.

For any of this to happen, you needed to see that this moment—this time together, this book—is your eye of the storm moment when you can make the changes to move in a new direction. You can, and will, stand strong in the storm and persevere to get the help you need and the time you want. We got the clarity you need to walk a different path without apology. You need to see the two paths available and choose stunningly successful—the path of the business owner.

You will seek to move further and further into your GENIUS and resist getting stuck in middle management, where you are involved in the tactical tasks you sought to delegate. You are a warrior for the standards, values, results, and promises your business makes to the world, and will seek the help to ensure you are elevating instead of struggling as you go forward. Once you have a strong base with unlicensed help, you will want to recruit other like-minded people to leverage the GENIUS of the team together in servicing and earning sales commissions.

Others recreate the wheel, losing time and money. You know the top team-building mistakes to avoid and the pitfalls that will cap your business if you build what a potential recruit wants versus what the business needs. By building with the right people, protecting and evolving as a business together, you will thrive in a performance culture where you do good work well as a collective, based on the heart of the business versus teams who perform to earn at all costs. This is the key to an abundance culture.

I shared openly about the times my business fell into a scarcity mindset, just as it has happened for my clients. Scarcity and security are costly. Leading yourself in abundance will ensure you can attract who you are at your core—not your GENIUS but your values—and attract others looking to grow versus earn money. This is the basis for synergy and growing together: each member using their unique GENIUS toward serving a common purpose.

We talked about the obstacles you will face and why it will be much harder to build on your own. To build a team successfully is to beat the odds, and yet we work with top producers who make this transition successfully every day. I think it is fair to say that trying to build a team solo, without support, is impossible. Trying to build with best in class support will have trying moments, but you are building versus talking and testing. The path was already tested, measured, and cleared for you.

You are your own magical recruitment fairy—except more of a Captain America, kick-butt-and-take-names type who insists on doing what you can working with what you have. Now is the time to promote yourself into the very role you dreamed about at the start of this book journey together. You are built to win, to conquer, to thrive. You have your wishes and dreams for a reason, and they brought us together to help you carve the path of your future.

The hero is you: When you step up. When you show up. When you refuse to back down. When you build it. You win. No one else has to walk in your shoes. No one else was there to rescue you when the world tested you. For me, through losing my marriage and my home; gaining a business six-figures in debt, later losing that first business; and treading very closely to compromising my second business, no one rescued me because the world wanted me to see and rescue myself.

The world is presenting you with an opportunity to grow because you are seeing an outdated, overworked, underpaid version of yourself. You are called to be more because, in a not so distant future, you already are more. Others might hesitate or question their capability, but you? You show up. You win. It is what you were built to do.

Ultimate leaders will not alter their values and principles for anyone or anything. They seek to constantly course-correct to a place where they are increasingly stronger, more whole, closer to their full selves. They peel away the layers and find an ideal prototype built for their unique missions. They know the shortcuts for money hold them back and can cost them their entire ability to have respect, influence, trust, and create safety for others to be open to work with their visions.

I wrote this book to connect with people. I wrote this book to expand from helping one team per thirty-minute interval to helping millions of people in sales-related industries worldwide. My ideal reader happens to be in real estate, but this book applies to all of our journeys expanding ourselves into teams and strong businesses. It applies to all of us who set out to help, to serve, and to contribute. It applies to those of us who built the dream only to find a new one, again and again and again. It applies to all of us who poured so much of our hearts into building something of value and sometimes lose ourselves along the way. It applies to those of us who looked around and suddenly realized that how we live matters, and what we do sets an example.

What we live and choose as an individual person, as a leader, as a family, and as a team is political. It matters, and with eyes watching us and our gaze being one of service, we finally realized that cheating ourselves out of our best lives—that selling out that top 1% life for the much lower destination of a top 1% business—is selling everyone else out with us. You are setting the example. You are setting the way. You, as a leader, now have a chance to set a new norm that includes you and establishes that you want others to have it all as much or more than you even care about having it for yourself.

I have a feeling if someone else were to lose out, you might hop into line and act faster. You might adjust to prove to that person what is possible. That is why I did it. I was willing to sacrifice myself for a greater good. I believed my life was worth more than my personal self for as long as I can remember being able to think. There was always an adventure to be had, an experience to create, an odd to be broken, and I happily stepped into the role of proving the peanut gallery wrong. If you are reading this book, I bet you beat the odds too. You overcame unbelievable challenges, you slayed dragons, and you sat in the deepest of despair; and yet, here you are, in the eye of the storm, about to build, about to level up, with the only calm moment you have.

You, my friend, are a warrior. You were built as a champion. You were built to win, and in building something with depth, the width of a solid foundation, and the resources for you to step into and truly live your best life—a Top 1% Life.

ACKNOWLEDGMENTS

There are so many people who I want to acknowledge in their assistance in the journey leading this book. First and foremost, I have to acknowledge my children. They know what it is to get things done at a pace that, I would guess, many other children or families, would not relate to experiencing on a daily basis. It has been me and my children growing together, as I sold real estate, coached, rebuilt one coaching business, built another new coaching business, and when I decided I wanted to hike and travel! My son has introduced me in front of hundreds of people at the Ultimate Team Summit. At that same event, he has volunteered for everything from registration to photography over the years. With no corporate sponsors, it was all us on the line, and that made Ultimate Team Summit a family affair. My son has reminded me that I am a whole lot of extra and has been there to say, "Mom, what's up with you? It is the final push, ground down, and get it done." My children have seen the toll of building events from scratch, going all in, without corporate sponsors or deep pockets. Family members have taken my daughter to auditions. And while I was traveling home from events and training, my daughter spent more afternoons doing homework alone than I would like to admit. My children and I are a dream team of all cooks, all in the kitchen, all at the same time, and yet we move mountains together. Under pressure, we all call rank, and heads duck, but it gets done! It takes a team and a village to run a business, raise children, and attempt any sort of a life. Before having my children I never really understood what a key role the children play in that village as they grow, learn, and mature. My children were not only raised by a village, they actively contributed to it.

Thank you to my sister. I think someone else said it best, "It has always been you and your sister, taking on the world." Love you, Val. Thank you for building unconditional love with me to lead our families back to wholeness, together. There is never a day that goes by when I am not thankful for you. I love you forever and will always have your back.

No team is strong without leaders, and we are blessed beyond words for our leadership team at Kathleen Black Coaching & Consulting Inc. I may be accused of expecting too much in terms of loyalty, honesty, results, overall good character, and entrepreneurial spirit from others. This team proved everyone who ever said I was unrealistic wrong. Our leadership team delivers more than I could ever ask, and more than money could ever buy. The truth is that they are the epitome of self-leadership creating a strong collective.

Special mention and love to Shannon Smith and Stacey Green. Thank you for believing in what we do and believing in me. Words could never say enough for how appreciated you are. You reminded me that what I always believed about the power of team did exist in my difficult moments of doubt.

Thank you to my best friends who put up with my ridiculous lack of availability, jump in and help with my children, have my back, go on my crazy adventures, even when they are scared of heights, and support me just the same because of it all. Liz and Donna, I love you both.

Thank you to my father Steven Black who passed at forty-one years old and left me with many gifts. He left me to appreciate time and life and taught me to give my best to every opportunity I choose to take. He always wondered what my life would look like if I applied myself. He only got to see the start of my adult life, luckily seeds are planted long before they flower.

Thank you to my Mother for taking on the world of the fire department, iron man, and side hustle of CPR instructor, dental assistant, and even Brownie leader. The idea that a woman could not lead never really crossed my mind. Perhaps I thought we did too much as women. Thank you for showing me that I did not need to have it all. I only needed to build what I wanted, my own way.

Thank you to my grandma and nanny for showing me what grace is, for picking me up when I was in trouble, often, and giving me a perfect balance of routine and freedom where I thrived. They took this world at its best despite what it may have given them, showing up strong every day. If they can face the things they did in this life, there is absolutely nothing I cannot face in mine. I still hear my grandmother's voice almost every day. She coaches me from heaven. As I write this acknowledgement my nanny is ninety-eight years old, and I will make a bet on her outsmarting all of us in almost anything.

My early clients took a risk on coaching with me as a new coach, and very shortly after, our whole coaching team and client family took a chance on coaching with a company led by me, when I was someone relatively new to the coaching industry. Some of us made magic together, reaching exceptional results. I will always be thankful for the trust you placed in me, and the chance you gave me to create those results with you. Those results continue to be the foundation of my company today. Thank you to so many clients: Rob Golfi, Cintia De Aguiar, Mike Boychuk, Justin Havre, Melissa Charlton, Chuck Charlton, Peggy Hill, Rob Johnstone, Aj Hazzi, Michael St. Jean, Teresa St. Jean, and Robin St. Jean, Tony Kalsi, Joe Pecharich & Christine Pecharich, Dan Gemus, Stan Bernardo, Rocco Manfredi, Mike Radcliffe, Jeremy Brooks, Angela Langtry, Melody May, Tom Joseph, Mike Heddle, Rina DiRisio, Wanda Westover, Rachel Hammer, Stacey Falkwin, Paul Germanese, Michael Christie, Emily Barry, and thousands of other agents and teams who trusted our guidance to coach in supporting their growth.

Thank you to all of the clients who coached with my coaching team and trainers. Names like Mark Faris, Drew Woolcott, Peggy Hill, Michael St Jean, Dan Gemus, Mike Heddle, Mary Wylde, Brad Wylde, Marla Simon, Stephen Simon, Stacey Falkwin, Melissa Charlton, Chuck Charlton, Sam McDadi, Amy Flowers, and so many more, have made a tremendous impact on our industry. They took a chance to build business in a new way. Names like these, and all of the leaders mentioned above prove teams really do, "do it better", every day. Over the years, I have heard of your progress, worked with our coaching team, or personally, worked on strategy to support you, and will always cheer you on. We are so grateful for the trust given and the opportunity to be part of your team now, or in the past.

Thank you to Dan Plowman for giving me the chance to develop the on boarding training program which allowed us to hit conversion and performance heights never achieved before with new agents. This work began a domino effect where we would exceed our company baselines with new content and a new approach through our coaching clients. For the faith in training the Dan Plowman Team, the opportunity to turn around the coaching company, and in ultimately seeing that my vision required a new playing field. Dan Plowman Team Systems was my first taste of the responsibilities of business ownership, decision making, leadership, and working with my own team. The buck stopped at me. I am forever proud of my work there, and forever grateful for the opportunity.

Special thank you to our in house team at Kathleen Black Coaching & Consulting Inc., our coaching team, our sales team, our affiliates, and those who support us. When you live in high performance, you expect a lot. This team exceeds my expectations and inspire all of our KBCC family to new heights. Thank you. I wanted more than paid employees or contractors, I envisioned people who believed in each other, our clients, and the importance of fulfilling our vision in the future. I envisioned a team guided by the highest of intentions, and that is what we now have.

Thank you to everyone who has donated their time and expertise to making Ultimate Team Summit world-class and to supporting our clients with your expertise: Andrew Fogliato, David Greenspan (MC is a crazy undertaking at the level you deliver it! Hire this man if you need an MC), Micah Munro, David Jenkins, Danny Wood (Thank you for the awesome, random, notes of encouragement, that always arrived at the perfect time), Ryan Hodge, Ado Topuz, and so many more.

I extend a thank you to all of the brokers who hired me, complained about my prices, saw agent results, and then hired us again! All true stories aside, I need to make a few special expressions of gratitude. Paul Baron runs the largest, highest performing, C21 brokerage in the entire country. I notice in our clients that good people do exceptionally well, and from everything I have witnessed, Paul Baron is a good person. I always teach about learning to be very selective with who I give my ear to for advice, who I take compliments from with a grain of salt, and who I brace myself to meet, knowing they will give direct, honest feedback on the good and on what could be better. Paul is a rare voice of honest and direct feedback and a broker who took a risk on me when I first left my prior coaching company. I have worked with C21 Leading Edge in training ever since. Years later, I still commend Paul Baron and his team, for being pro-team in supporting their agents, creating team advantages available to all agents in the brokerage, and seeking experts in various areas of the real estate industry. Thank you for your trust, taking a chance on me, your unfiltered feedback, and leading the way for so many in this industry.

There have been several brokers who have supported my inhouse training programs and my business expansion. I still remember feeling caught off guard when Nelson Goulart reached out to help me for apparently no reason. He was the first mirror of a real estate world, not quite as harsh as some would have us believe. Nelson has attended Ultimate Team Summit annually and supported our training programs for his agents. Thank you, Nelson. Your values are so needed in this industry.

Peter Campoli, Alex Ocsai, Gloria Riddall, Rajeef Koneswaran, Rhonda Best, Tim Syrianos, Jen O'Brien, Amy Youngren: Thank you to all of the Real Estate Boards who work hard for our Industry and invest in speakers like me to share our work with the world, RealtorQuest, REALiTY Conference, Janice Parish, Andrew Zsolt, Ron McIntosh, Banff Real Estate Connection, Bill Madder, and Merrily Hackett.

C21 Canada put me on my first National stage as the featured Mainstage Keynote. You do not get to those stages without people taking risks on you. We can, and I believe we do, have an unmatched track record for team building success and results. That does not change that someone is taking a chance to put you on a bigger stage with their event on the line. C21 Canada also placed their trust in us to support the pro-team mentality for their brokers, and in supporting team growth for team leaders. Thank you, and I am grateful for the relationship with your team.

Thank you to Barry Lebow for taking his time to write an article on our work, to *REM* and *REP* magazine for the consistent support in publishing my articles. Thank you to *REP* for putting me on your event stage and for twice selecting me as one of the "Top Women in Real Estate". Thank you to T3 Sixty for surprising me by selecting me as one of the Top 20 Emerging Leaders, in the 2018 Swanepoel Report.

Thank you to Angela Lauria and The Author Incubator's team, as well as to David Hancock and the Morgan James Publishing team for helping me bring this book to print.

Thank you to everyone in the future who supports our message by investing in the power of team for their community. We are only speakers when blessed with audiences. We are only coaches when blessed with clients. We are only leaders when blessed with the courage to grow and share, while being humble enough to also stay forever as students. I am truly grateful. Thank you.

THANK YOU

I am so thankful that we got to go on this journey together. I am excited to hear your success and to continue cheering you on. I know you will move forward, taking action to build the life and business you deserve! As a way of thanking you for reaching out and sharing your progress with me, I would love to offer you more support! As a gift to extend our journey, I am offering you a free sixty-minute class on organizing your sales business so you have time for a life, to get everything organized, and to have time for your family.

To get your free copy, first share your review about the book, and go to my website: www.ItTakesa.Team/Top1PercentLife

You can also access a free business assessment and request a complimentary strategy call with our team while you are there!

I would love to keep in touch with you. You can follow me to stay in touch. I have added my social media and contact details here:

Personal Facebook: https://www.facebook.com/kathleen.black.3158
Kathleen Black Coaching & Consulting
Website: www.ItTakesa.Team
Email: info@KathleenSpeaks.com
Facebook: https://www.facebook.com/KathleenBlackCoaching/
Ultimate Team Summit Facebook: https://www.facebook.com/ultimateteamsummit
Instagram: https://www.instagram.com/kathleenblackcoaching/
Linkedin: https://www.linkedin.com/in/kathleen-black-4811a052/

ABOUT THE AUTHOR

 Kathleen Black is North America's leading real estate team coach. Delivering her proven success techniques, behind the most efficient, productive, and profitable real estate sales business's globally. That growth is worth billions in additional sales volume annually across her client network, with 80% of her clients being national top 1% producers. Kathleen will help you to expand your business at a fraction of the time and cost using the tried, tested, and true "KBCC Ultimate Expansion Strategy" that powers her client growth.

The success of KBCC centers around integrity, honesty, and results-driven measures, the very things that represent Kathleen.

Kathleen was named twice as Top 100 Elite Women Driving the Future of Real Estate by REP Magazine and as one of Top 20 Emerging Leaders by T3 Sixty's 2018 Swanepoel Report. She was recognized within the top 1% of Realtors in the Toronto Real Estate Board, has ten-plus years of agent development experience, and hundreds of teams attribute their growth and success to Kathleen's leadership.

Kathleen is also the driving-force behind the Ultimate Team Summit, the largest team specific real estate related sales summit in North America and the Ultimate Mastermind Series of events, including the Top 1% Ultimate Mastermind.

Kathleen lives in Oshawa, Ontario, Canada, with her two free spirited, independent, and very-loved children Ethan and Ella, and their cat Ethel.

Printed in the USA
CPSIA information can be obtained
at www.ICGtesting.com
JSHW022327140824
68134JS00019B/1344